Spooky Creepy Boston

Spooky Creepy Boston

Nicholas Goodwin

Schiffer Publishing Ltd®

4880 Lower Valley Road, Atglen, Pennsylvania 19310

Often in the telling, "legend tripping" involves exaggeration or the idea of trespass. This is not appropriate behavior for scholars and lovers of folklore. Please always get permission before going on anyone's private property in the name of investigating spooky or creepy places. Always.

Schiffer Books are available at special discounts for bulk purchases for sales promotions or premiums. Special editions, including personalized covers, corporate imprints, and excerpts can be created in large quantities for special needs. For more information contact the publisher:

Published by Schiffer Publishing Ltd.
4880 Lower Valley Road
Atglen, PA 19310
Phone: (610) 593-1777; Fax: (610) 593-2002
E-mail: Info@schifferbooks.com

For the largest selection of fine reference books on this and related subjects,
please visit our web site at **www.schifferbooks.com**
We are always looking for people to write books on new and related subjects.
If you have an idea for a book please contact us at the above address.

This book may be purchased from the publisher.
Include $5.00 for shipping.
Please try your bookstore first.
You may write for a free catalog.

In Europe, Schiffer books are distributed by
Bushwood Books
6 Marksbury Ave.
Kew Gardens
Surrey TW9 4JF England
Phone: 44 (0) 20 8392-8585; Fax: 44 (0) 20 8392-9876
E-mail: info@bushwoodbooks.co.uk
Website: www.bushwoodbooks.co.uk

All text and photos by authors unless otherwise noted
Never again the burning. *Photo courtesy of Jayna Lloyd of Jayna Sullivan Photography.*
It is amazing what people can convince themselves that they believe. *Photo courtesy of Jayna Lloyd of Jayna Sullivan Photography*
Mental illness is a problem in and of itself, but the haunted asylums of Massachusetts have spawned legends of problems far worse than madness. *Photo courtesy of Jayna Lloyd of Jayna Sullivan Photography.*

Designed by Mark David Bowyer
Type set in Viner Hand ITC / New Baskerville BT

ISBN: 978-0-7643-3612-6
Printed in the United States of America

Contents

Acknowledgments

Chase DeNamur

Renee Des Anges

Caitlin R. Kiernan

Mike Krausert

Natasha Kraven

Jayna Lloyd

Justine Pierotti

Kathryn Pollnac

Dr. Faye Ringel

Haley Wright

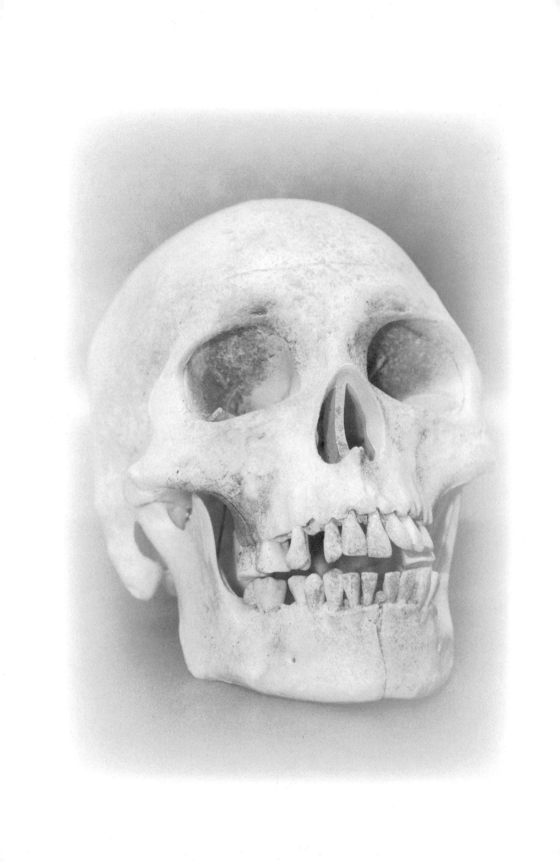

Introduction

Called the "Athens of America," Boston, Massachusetts, is a center of American history and culture. The ancient city was the crucible of the American Revolution, and many of the buildings where America's Founders met to chart the course of the young nation still stand to this very day. Boston and its immediate suburbs (Brookline, Cambridge, and Somerville) are today home to over fifty colleges and universities, creating an unparalleled atmosphere of intellectual endeavor and technological innovation. The Charles River—one of the only urban rivers in the country dedicated purely to recreational use—winds through the metropolitan area, offering opportunities for sailing, rowing, and taking in some charming views. Boston is also home to America's largest Irish-American community and some of the wildest sports fanatics in the United States. Now that baseball's Red Sox broke the "Curse of the Bambino," by winning the World Series twice after an eighty-six year drought, and the New England Patriots shattered long-held records in football, "Beantown" is as well-known for its jocks as it is for its philosophers.

Any city as ancient as Boston, and with as many illustrious residents and places, and with a seedy underbelly as large as Boston's, will also have its share of ghosts, haunted sites, murderers, and madmen. I was not born in Boston, but was always attracted to it. Unlike the other great cities of the Northeast—New York (where I am from) and Philadelphia, Boston never let go of its past. The other cities have been rewritten, but Boston is known for never even having fully adapted its roadways to the automobile. A line in the otherwise forgettable horror film *Warlock* is both apt and telling. In the film, seventeenth century witch-hunter Redferne finds himself on the trail of the titular warlock in modern-day Los Angeles and Boston. Boston, there are "turns of corner" he recognizes; Tremont Street is familiar to him, despite a gap of three hundred years.

The history of the Boston area is the history of America. Salem never could separate itself from the horrors of the witch trials, and ultimately embraced their dark legacy, transforming itself into the "Witch City." There are the suburban mental hospitals where life was cheap and where the spirits of the damned wandered subterranean tunnels; now they are suburban condominium complexes, but the gothic silhouettes of the original buildings still stand tall on windswept hills. Cape Cod is the home of long-dead witches, one of America's only female serial killers, and the horror of a woman drowning while a Senator swam for freedom. Then there is Boston proper—its haunted jails transformed into luxury hotels, its parks loaded with the bodies of the hanged, the forts and lighthouses where the ghosts of the city's protectors (and its fierce enemies) never quite left.

Boston and its suburbs—which stretch from Salem in the north to Ashland in the Metrowest, has had more than three centuries of religious fervor, desperate women, haughty aristocrats, and some people who just one day *snap*. There is the Boston of the World Series and Harvard Yard, and there is a spooky, creepy Boston as well. This Boston, and its eerie environs, are what attract ghost hunters, thrill seekers, and even thoughtful people who hope that America can be spared another era of hysteria and witch hunts. For these people, for you, I have written this book.

Nicholas Goodwin,
Boston, Massachusetts

Chapter One
Truth and Mother Goose

It has been assumed, tacitly and avowedly, directly and indirectly, that the ultimate object of all Poetry is Truth. Every poem, it is said, should inculcate a moral; and by this moral is the poetical merit of the work to be adjudged. We Americans especially have patronized this happy idea; and we Bostonians, very especially, have developed it in full. We have taken it into our heads that to write a poem simply for the poem's sake, and to acknowledge such to have been our design, would be to confess ourselves radically wanting in the true Poetic dignity and force:—but the simple fact is, that, would we permit ourselves to look into our own souls, we should immediately there discover that under the sun there exists nor can exist any work more thoroughly dignified—more supremely noble than this very poem—this poem per se—this poem which is a poem and nothing more—this poem written solely for the poem's sake.

—Edgar Allan Poe
"The Poetic Principle," 1849

Jack and Jill went up the hill, To draw a pail of water; Jack fell down and broke his crown, And Jill came tumbling after.
—A Mother Goose Nursery Rhyme, 1833

Boston and Massachusetts, more so than any other city and state in the United States of America's history, is the nation's birthplace. One of the lesser-known "births" is that of Mother Goose in the United States. Like with folklorists and those who accumulate haunted legends, Mother Goose is often seen as a collector, or even an author. Rhymes and stories change a bit, and rearrange, when they are told out loud and Mother

Goose even appears as a character in her "own" stories. Whether we picture her as a large goose in a hat and shawl or a dowdy and bespectacled grandmother, the character and the stories will remain forever inseparable.

Folklore does not have an archetypal collector, but it would help if there were one. The characters and settings are specific yet they also change to fit the story that needs to be told. Boston, of anywhere in the country, embodies this process of shifting stories most of all because Mary Goose (d. 1690, 42 years old), often rumored to be the very first "Mother Goose," is buried in Boston in the Granary Burying Ground on Tremont Street. The character dates back to France in the 1650s, but the story has taken hold in ways that make "Mother Goose" real and buried in Boston. Then again, another "true" Boston story says that Mother Goose was named Elizabeth Foster Goose and died in 1758. A historian and travel writer of the 1930s and 1940s, Eleanor Early, stated another "truth," that Mother Goose lived in Boston in the 1660s.

All three of these women have been purported to be married to a man named Isaac Goose (or perhaps it was Isaac Vergoose or Isaac Vertigoose) who had been previously married. In these stories, Mother Goose and Isaac Goose meet and become a family with a total of sixteen children between them. It is the way that they became the "Goose Bunch." Sometimes, especially in the Eleanor variations, Isaac dies and Mother Goose takes the children to what was once Pudding Lane (and is now Devonshire Street) to live with the husband of the eldest Goose daughter, the publisher Thomas Fleet. Eventually, with the Goose children, grandchildren, and the kids of the neighborhood hanging on the words of Mother Goose's stories, her publisher son-in-law had no choice but to collect and publish her stories and nursery rhymes. Other scholars have traced Mother Goose to be an incarnation of the wife of France's King Robert II, saying that his wife was a beloved and revered storyteller known as *Berthe pied d'oie* ("Goose-Footed Bertha"). Until Charles Perrault published a collection of tales subtitled "Contes de ma mère l'Oye" ("Tales of my Mother Goose"), there is no certain starting point. In 1729, there was a British translation of the Perrault collection. Then, in 1765, there was a British collection of nursery rhymes. In Worcester, Massachusetts, the first American edition of Mother Goose was from printer Isiah Thomas reprinting that British collection. From there seems to be the starting point for all the other versions of the story that incorporate Boston.

The stories of *Spooky, Creepy Boston* are no different. The Commonwealth of Massachusetts is a port city for folktales and ghost stories. Massachusetts takes the stories of New England and the embrace of the Atlantic Ocean and those mingling tales cross the lips of the over six million people who live in Massachusetts. As Boston is the "Athens of America," it is also the "Cradle of Liberty." Plymouth was the second permanent settlement the British planted on North America. Throughout the 1620s and 1630s, perhaps just before the birth of the legend of Mother Goose, the colonists built towns throughout Massachusetts. A century and a half later, those same towns were where the desire for independence from Great Britain began to ignite.

In the same way that Boston inspired the America Revolution, Massachusetts was also the first state to abolish the practice of slavery. Before the first gunshot of the Civil War, abolitionists and the leaders of the temperance movement were headquartered in Massachusetts. Trading with Europe, fishing and agriculture led to being a hub of manufacturing during the Industrial Revolution. Today, Eastern Massachusetts plays a major role in American higher education, technology, and health care.

By being at the innermost point of the Massachusetts Bay and at the mouth of the Charles River, the stories of Boston have swept across Massachusetts. Massachusetts is a state with lingering pockets of old growth forests. Before their extinction over the last two or three hundred years, elk, wolverines, mountain lions and gray wolves inhabited the places off of the beaten paths. The legends contained in this volume are no different. The majority of the people in Massachusetts live within sixty miles of Boston and most of the spooky and creepy stories start there as well.

Boston and the eerie environs of Massachusetts are more than steaming clam chowder or the cold night air of late October. Boston is home to terrifying spirits and ghosts. This collection contains the most prominent of these tales—but Boston's history is alive everywhere. Ghosts lurk in every boneyard. Every place is haunted. Be it the paranormal presences set loose by the public noose-danglings in Boston Common, such as in 1660 when Mary Dyer and three other Quakers were hanged by the neck until dead for practicing their religion, or from the dark deeds of more recent events, every place is haunted.

This is the spooky, creepy Boston that should be shared with all the world. Another wonderfully shocking tale of early Massachusetts history is demonstrated by how founding father, the Governor of the Colony, Richard Bellingham, in the Spring of 1651, made the heads of the Puritans spin when he married a woman less than half his age and performed the ceremony all by himself. He had just been elected and was fifty years old. His bride, Penelope Pelham, the niece of the Lord de la Warr, who the state of Delaware is named after, was twenty-one. Remarrying was not unusual. Governor John Winthrop was widowed three times. Penelope Pelham's grandfather, Herbert Pelham, had a second marriage that made Penelope's aunt into her step-grandmother, but young Penelope was about to become engaged to a friend of Governor Bellingham's who was her own age. The man's name is lost but it is known that he was living in the Governor's home at the time. Governor Bellingham watched Penelope date the young man living in his home and found that he wanted her all to himself. Before anyone knew, even though both custom and law dictated that the intention to marry be announced publicly, Governor Bellingham tied the rope of the wedding knot with his own hands. Charges were brought against him, but Richard Bellingham insisted that he, as Governor, should automatically be allowed to judge his own trial. John Winthrop tries to explain that loophole away by saying that Governor Bellingham was excused for his behavior, "by the strength of his affection, and that she was not absolutely promised to the other gentleman." Somehow, Winthrop's explanation does not explain away Governor Bellingham's actions.

Thus, it is proven that Boston has always been both spooky and creepy.

Scholars of folklore struggle with how legends should be defined and categorized. Fantastical tales and fact-based legends are separated from each other, but it always remains hard to tell the difference between stories that might be partially true and stories that cannot hold a grain of truth. Controversies abound with darkly delightful stories such as these. False stories are often said to be true when they are told. What has happened is that "legends" have come to be the stories that are believed by the tellers but that are not believed by the folklorist. This determination is usually made by applying standards of objective truth, examining the way the tale is told and assessing how convinced the teller is that their story is true.

Any astute reader can easily see that all of these distinctions are muddy hogwash. The ability to differentiate objective truth is bestowed on folklorists, as if those who collect these tales are somehow inherently sane. There is no way to prove a ghostly touch or a person rapidly rotting before one's eyes to be untrue.

Someone walking this earth believes every possible thing. Wide eyes can mean surprise or incredulity, but they can also mean rapt and quivering excitement. What a person says and what they believe have nothing to do with that which is real or can be proven. The internet is home to madness and speculation that was once confined to America's small towns and isolated communities. Now, even enlightened city folk can become enamored with the most cockamamie of ideas. Folk beliefs are no more or less false than the bizarre assertion that folklorists do not drool, huddle in corners or see dancing specters that cannot possibly be there.

Legends are willing to go places where they are not supposed to go, just like the people who play roles in the stories. Fragmented and open-ended rambles are the nature of legends and folklore and the compilations of legends and folklore. Where are we, as people in Boston or people of the world, going but to dark, despicable and altogether hideous places where we should never ever desire to be? If we are not marching to doom and gloom, why are so many ghosts screaming?

Stories are art and ghost stories are often Outsider art. Folklorists collect folk beliefs the way that music lovers adore strange visionaries who emerge from a world outside of traditional music. Superstitions are more than entertainment to be typed up for amusement. Centuries of wisdom are presented as anecdotal evidence. One of the most inspiring stories in the history of rock and roll is that Dot, Helen, and Betty Wiggins. The three lovely sisters are known as The Shaggs. They grew up, as impoverished as could be, in New Hampshire. With the help of their father, Austin Wiggins, they recorded an album, in Massachusetts, that was almost lost in the sands of time. (Which, one well knows, would scratch a record quite badly because sand and vinyl grooves should not mix.) The debut album by The Shaggs, *Philosophy of the World*, was recorded in a single day. Less than one hundred copies of the thousand pressings were available to buy because the Third World (its name, it was not outside of the United States) record label went under as the record was released. Yet we are able to listen to their music today because of the conservation efforts of music lovers.

This is the nature of folklore. We keep alive that which is special or unique about that which we value most. So much dark history lurks in Boston! Fort Warren on Georges Island, the Omni Parker House Hotel, the Majestic Theater, and the tragic and harrowing events of Salem's witch trials are revealed here for the dark legends that they have become. This book is a guide for ghost hunters. It is a retelling of words that have crossed generations' worth of lips. It is a metaphorical journey into the depths of dungeons and jails. Here is to hoping that everyone finds a narrow secret passageway or hears strange caterwauling that they have never heard before.

It is all real. Every blade and every mark. Every conspiracy. Demons, no demons. Ghosts, no ghosts. We are surrounded by all of them and the lack of them. This is because, like gravity or the weather, there are forces in the world that are far greater than humans can understand and there are forces that are not good and forces that are not evil. This may be because good and evil do not exist. This is not an exit. It is an acknowledgement that everything is far more complicated than I have ever imagined. This makes it likely that everything is far more complicated than you, too, have ever imagined—because I have imagined a great deal about spooky, creepy Boston...

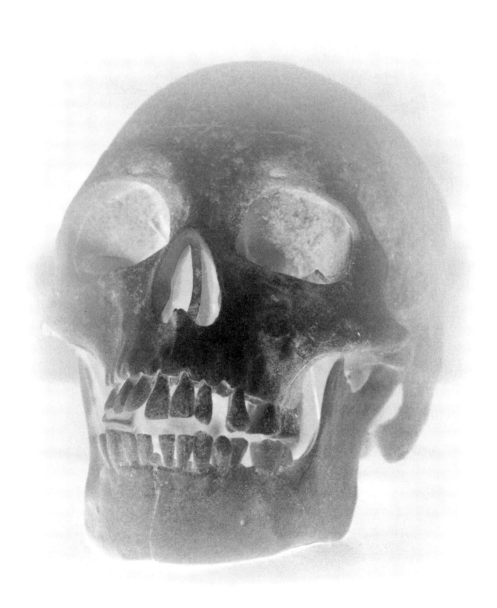

Chapter Two
Boston

A Classic Boston Ghost Story: Mrs. Ess

A classic Boston ghost story that even appeared in the *New York Times* in 1888 is particularly representative of the form because it has the traditional touches of the haunted stories that were prevalent in that earlier era. In the way that the tale was told in the *Times*, a popular and well-liked family named the Esses always spent summers in their beautiful summer home on the North Shore. They were a well-to-do and well-liked family. Along with wealth and prestige, the Esses were known for gallivanting and socializing.

As the paper reported the story, Mrs. Ess—a vivacious, well-spoken, and elegant woman—died suddenly during a brief visit to Hartford, Connecticut. She had been feeling unwell, struggling with a case of pneumonia, but the family and Mrs. Ess were convinced that she was on the mend. On that fateful day of her passing, in what seemed like an arbitrary coincidence, the family's personal physician stopped by the Ess family's expansive summer home on the North Shore. The physician stopped by because he had known that Mrs. Ess had been sick and he wanted to check on her condition.

The youngest daughter of the Ess clan told the physician that a long letter from his patient had arrived. The young daughter found the letter, which was in her sick mother's handwriting, and showed the physician. The daughter pointed to the spot in the letter that explained that her mother, Mrs. Ess, was feeling much better than she had previously. Mrs. Ess had written that she expected to overcome her malady by the day that the letter from Hartford would arrive at the family home in Boston. Since the letter had just arrived, Mrs. Ess was presumed to be the picture of health.

As the physician rose from his chair, he thanked the young girl for the good news about her mother. As the physician then exited the house through the front door, he was surprised to see Mrs. Ess dash across the front lawn. The physician shook his head as he watched her duck into her home through a side door. It seemed odd that Mrs. Ess passed within twenty feet of him yet seemed not to even notice that he was there. He decided to investigate because it was unlike her to not have acknowledged a guest in any way.

The physician ran back in through the front door—but no one else in the building had seen or heard Mrs. Ess at all. The door that the doctor claimed Mrs. Ess had entered through was clearly and demonstrably locked from the inside. As the doctor continued insisting, more and more loudly, that he was certain that he had seen Mrs. Ess only a moment before, a telegram arrived that informed the family of the sad news that Mrs. Ess had died less than an hour previous, still one hundred miles away in Hartford.

The Lady in Black

The story of the Lady in Black (sometimes called more simply the Black Lady) dates to when Fort Warren—a twenty-eight acre edifice on Georges Island at the mouth of Boston Harbor, was a prison for the North that was used to hold Southern prisoners of war during Civil War. Though designed to protect the harbor, the cannons of Fort Warren never fired upon enemy ships. Instead, it was a POW camp and held not only rebel soldiers but local Confederate sympathizers and even some elected officials from the breakaway state of Maryland. Fort Warren was well-suited for the task, with its dungeons, moat, and tunnels that should have made the prison impregnable. Today, they all serve as reminders of the horrors of the Civil War and the Lady in Black.

Thrusting their sharp points at the sky, these wrought iron decorations make even a typical Beacon Hill brownstone seem heavy with a sense of foreboding.

Little is known about the exact historical roots of the story. The most common story is that her name was Melanie Lanier, and she was married to a soldier, Samuel (though some sources list his name as Andrew), who was imprisoned in Fort Warren. Melanie sneaked to Boston all the way from the Confederacy. Once in Boston, she met with family friends who lived in nearby Hull and put her plan to work. Melanie would have likely made a better soldier than Samuel, and was certainly a superior spy. She used a telescope to chart the changing of the guard and the daily schedule of the prisoners. Then, on one sleet-filled night, she cut her hair, clothed herself in the uniform of a Union soldier and, disguised as a man, rowed her boat across the Boston Harbor to reach the fort.

She stayed disguised and hidden as she searched for her lost husband. It is most often said that Melanie's husband was one of the prisoners taken by General Burnside after her husband—whom it is often said that she married only weeks before—was kidnapped at Roanoke Island. Samuel had been allowed to correspond with his wife, and he was expecting her. She whistled a song they both knew—though it's unclear how such a tune could have been heard over the driving sleet of a Boston winter— and soon a rope of bedclothes and scraps was lowered to Melanie. She climbed up to the prisoner's barracks with a sack that contained a pick, small shovel, and an aging pistol. However, the other prisoners were not satisfied with the idea of the two lovebirds leaving. They seized the material and hatched a far more audacious plan—dig to the armory, appropriate weapons, seize the fort and a ship, then sail to freedom.

Melanie is said to have lived hidden among the prisoners for two weeks as dirt was shifted and walls cracked. However, the plan was discovered and the conspirators brought before fort commander Colonel Dimmick. Melanie had still managed to hang on to her pistol.

The story here branches into several different versions—some say that Samuel was killed by guards when Melanie was caught and some say that his mortal wound was caused by his wife's gun misfiring during the shoot out with the prison guards.

Regardless of the cause of his death, Melanie's husband was dead by the time that his wife was sentenced to hang on February 7, 1862. She expressed the wish that she wanted to die dressed as a woman and not disguised as a man. Because there were no other women on the island, there were no women's clothes to be found. It is said that Melanie Lanier, the proud Confederate woman who had found her husband only to lose him again, was marched to the gallows wearing black cloth salvaged from either mess hall drapes or a burial shroud.

As if lit only by gaslight, these brick colonial buildings show off Beacon Hill's cobblestones.

As one would guess, Melanie lives on. Soon after, the story goes, a soldier named Richard Cassidy was nearly strangled by the Lady in Black. When Fort Warren was still used as a fort, unusual events were frequently reported by the soldiers. Just before the outbreak of the First World War, a soldier heard loud voices giving him instructions not to enter the area of the fort that was known as the Corridor of Dungeons. Soldiers have also been known to flee their posts or fire their guns in the air when ghostly figures suddenly materialized right before their eyes. It is said that one soldier spent his final days in a mental hospital after an encounter with the vengeful Melanie Lanier.

The belief is, of course, that the Lady in Black is the cause of all of these ghostly activities. Unlike most ghost sightings, which are often tied to a specific geographical area where a death trauma was experienced, the Lady in Black is seen throughout the Boston area. Trying to free her husband, failing and being hanged appears to have unleashed a peculiar sort of vengeance that haunts Fort Warren and the surrounding areas. The Lady in Black has even been seen walking the streets of Boston in her black robes.

Fort Warren is now a tourist area, as is all of Georges Island—which also features picnic areas, interesting tidal pools, a free ferry shuttle to other nearby islands (though the ferry from the shore requires a fee) and a dock for small private boats. Open 9AM till sunset, and open three seasons a year—no chance to reenact Melanie Lanier's daring raid during the winter months—Georges Island and Fort Warren can make for a pleasant day trip. Just don't plan to stay after dark.

Boston Harbor Island Visitors' Guide: http://www. bostonislands.org/isle_georges.asp

Ferry service: (617) 223-8666

Private mooring reservations: (617) 241-9640 or moorings@bosport.com

The Boston Strangler

Anna E. Slesers, sexually molested and strangled with the cord from her bathrobe.

Nina Nichols, sexually molested and strangled with a pair of her own nylons.

Helen Blake, sexually molested and strangled with a pair of her own nylons.

Jane Sullivan, sexually molested and strangled with a pair of her own nylons.

They were older women, not floozies or tramps, and these were just a few of the victims of a man who may still be alive to this very day. In the summer of 1962, the Boston Strangler was on the prowl, and it seemed that no female was safe. The killer was frantic—two victims, Nichols and Blake, were found on June 30th. But when summer ended, so too did the slayings. For a few months.

Then after months of inactivity, the killer seemed to strike again. On the 5th of December, Sophie Clark was found dead, having been assaulted and then strangled with a pair of her own nylons. Yet she was young, twenty-one, African-American, and lived with roommates unlike the older women who had been attacked that summer. Between the end of 1962 and the beginning of 1964, eight more women were to be killed, most in the same way, for a total of thirteen slayings. Two, the sixty-nine-year-old Mary Brown and Beverly Samans, twenty-three, were stabbed to death and some believe those two to be victims of another murderer. Others, including the Boston police of the era, believe that Samans—an aspiring opera singer—was stabbed by the Strangler only after a failed attempt at strangulation. Her throat muscles were just too strong for even a grown man to compress with his bare hands, or so the story goes.

Nobody knows how many women the Strangler ultimately killed, and indeed nobody knows who he was. The term "serial killer" had yet to be coined in the early 1960s, and profiling and other techniques commonly used today were in their infancy. Desperate after the seemingly inexplicable Clarke and Samans murders of the spring of 1963, the police turned to a self-proclaimed psychic named Paul Gordon. Gordon described the Strangler as "as fairly tall, [man] bony hands, pale white skin, red, bony knuckles, his eyes hollow-set." He was likely from Maine or Vermont, and had an obsession with his mother, Gordon said. Gordon then selected mental patient Arnold Wallace from a set of mug shots. Wallace, whom Gordon had correctly indicated to be "in a hospital or some kind of home" was a mental patient who frequently escaped from the hospital in which he was being held. Some of the dates of his escape matched likely murder dates. It was uncanny, too uncanny. The police investigated Gordon and found that he had visited the hospital prior to offering up his "visions." Had he seen Wallace on the grounds? For his part, Wallace had a very low IQ and an inability to tell fact and fantasy apart. He was given a lie detector test and was returned to the hospital.

Then, on September 8, 1963, in the nearby town of Salem, Evelyn Corbin, 58, was found strangled with her own nylons. On November 25th, in the suburb of Lawrence, Joann Graff, 23, was found strangled with her nylons. There would be one more murder as well—another young girl, Mary Lawrence was found on January 4, 1964, strangled with a stocking and violated with the handle of a broomstick. Two weeks later, the Massachusetts Attorney General took over the case.

Finally, the case seemingly broke with a confession. Albert DeSalvo had a record. He even had nicknames. As The Measuring Man, he had been found guilty of passing himself off as a scout for a modeling agency. He would go door-to-door and tell attractive young women that their names had been given to the agency for which he worked, and that he was there to take their measurements. He also engaged in some other minor crime, and was known as a man with an immense sexual appetite. In November 1964, he was arrested after breaking into a home, tying a woman up, and fondling her. Before anything else happened, though, he appeared to have a change of heart and quietly left. The police sketch made, based on the woman's report, reminded police of the Measuring

Man. DeSalvo was brought in and when his mug shot was sent around to police departments across New England, he was also identified as the Green Man—a rapist wanted across neighboring Connecticut whose nickname came from the green work pants the assailant wore. DeSalvo admitted to hundreds of break-ins and some rapes and was sent to Bridgewater State Hospital for observation. Dr. Ames Robey, who first interviewed DeSlavo at Bridgewater, claimed that DeSalvo confessed to assaulting six hundred women, and later upped that count to one thousand.

DeSalvo was considered a nice guy by many who knew him, but his wife was not surprised when he was named as a suspect in sex crimes. However, there was also wide agreement about something else: DeSalvo was a blowhard, a confabulator, a liar. Little is known of his childhood, though his father was surely abusive and had battered Albert's mother. Some sources even claim that Albert and his sister were sold into slavery as children, but escaped. He even had a motivation to confess to the Strangler murders, or to have his friend in Bridgewater, George Nassar, do it for him. There was a $10,000 reward for information leading to an arrest, and in these days before the "Son of Sam" law kept criminals from profiting from their crimes, Nassar and DeSalvo could split the money. DeSalvo also seems to have believed that the reward was $10,000 per *victim*, which would have solved his money troubles for life. All he had to do was plead insanity, and he would avoid the death penalty and keep his family fed indefinitely. And DeSalvo had legendary attorney F. Lee Bailey on his side. Bailey was also the attorney for George Nassar, who was in prison for murdering a gas station attendant.

DeSalvo's confessions filled fifty tapes and 2,000 pages of transcriptions. The gory, exhausting details checked out. DeSalvo even confessed to an attempted murder nobody knew about. He had his hands on her when a glance in the mirror shocked him to sanity. He apologized, begged the woman not to tell, and then left. With DeSalvo's confession to go on, the woman was found by the police, interviewed, and indeed the story checked out.

And yet…

Even today, DeSalvo has his defenders. There's not a shred of physical evidence connecting him to any of the murder sites. Perhaps had DNA testing been feasible in the early 1960s, there would have been. There were some things DeSalvo got wrong; he claimed, for example, to have had intercourse with Mary Sullivan, but there was no physical evidence of any sexual contact. Indeed, in 2001, the bodies of Sullivan and DeSalvo were exhumed and analysis of DNA by James Starrs, professor of forensic science at George Washington University confirmed that DeSalvo did not have intercourse with Sullivan.

Further, a number of people saw "the Strangler" entering and leaving the residences of his victims—none of the descriptions given by witnesses matched DeSalvo. However, a woman who lived in the same building as young Sophie Clark did recognize George Nassar, DeSalvo's Bridgewater bunkmate. DeSalvo had a good memory and could have pieced together information from the copious press leaks, could have even been fed details by police eager to close the case, and then there was his roommate.

And of course, given what we know today of profiling, the idea of a single murderer killing both young women and old, treating some of the corpses with relative "kindness" and others as the target of sexualized rage doesn't quite fit what the average serial killer would do. DeSalvo was never put on trial for the Strangler murders, but instead was convicted of the Green Man sexual assaults. He escaped prison, but was quickly recaptured and sent to Walpole State Prison. In November of 1973, DeSalvo reached out to his old contact from Bridgewater, forensic psychologist Dr. Ames Robey. DeSalvo promised to tell Robey who the Strangler really was, and seemed quite nervous. With good reason too. DeSalvo was dead by morning—a knife in the heart.

This is not a ghost story, but the tale of the Boston Strangler is certainly a creepy one. DeSalvo is long dead, and the murders have stopped…or at least women don't wear nylons so often anymore. Albert's brother Richard DeSalvo has spent years trying to prove Albert's innocence, even going to significant lengths to keep Albert's body preserved in case of an exhumation like the one that cleared Albert of the Sullivan rape in 2001. There may have been more than one Strangler, which suggests that one or more serial killers may still be at large. Writer Susan Kelly contends that fully half-a-dozen murderers were operating on the streets on Boston and the surrounding suburbs during the years of the murders, and we know now that serial killers don't stop unless they are stopped by prison, execution, or some other form of death or incapacity. For his part, George Nassar, who is still alive as of this writing and is still serving a life sentence in prison for murder, has denied any role in the Strangler slayings.

The Charles Street Jail (The Liberty Hotel)

It is surprising that Boston does not have a greater number of haunted jails. Across the United States, tales of misconduct from both sides of the steel bars are a frequent source of hauntings, or at least tales of the same. The one legend that does persist in Boston is that of the Charles Street Jail. In the front yard of the Charles Street Jail, many were executed. Referred to as the Suffolk County Jail for a period of time, the Charles Street Jail has held the famous and the infamous alike, including the controversial figures of Sacco and Vanzetti, Italian anarchists who may have been as innocent as anyone can be and yet, even after an international political movement to free them, were still hanged for a robbery and murder they did not commit.

Down this dark alley, with gothic shadows, lies an iron gate.

Other parts of Boston make it clear that it is a vibrant city, the hub of New England.

The Charles Street Jail has a picturesque view of the Charles River and is near Beacon Hill, but it is also considered dangerously haunted ground. Perhaps in an attempt to hide the many government-sanctioned deaths and the legacy of crime and captivity, the jail has now been turned, in what can only be seen as a delicious instance of irony, into the Liberty Hotel. The renovations have made a point of keeping the historical look of the hotel. Not only do the great stone walls of the hotel continue to intimidate, the interior keeps the tier architecture of the old prison. From the lobby, guests and staff can be seen walking the open-air hallways and entering the rooms, just as prisoners did for more than a century. Though the renovations, of course, involved removing most of the bars and cells, the area is almost certainly still haunted by the prisoners who lived and died on the spot. It is a testament to the jail's memory that some of the cells have been left in place despite the building having been converted into a hotel.

Notorious criminals were kept there from 1851 up through 1990 and the hotel has only been open for a few years. Not enough time has passed to bury its new purposes beneath its old. Now as the Liberty Hotel, the former Charles Street Jail is known for being haunted year round but its legacy is most celebrated in October. Halloween is when the Nightmare on Charles Street festival often occurs. Some say the party is little more than a ghoulish and drunken party thrown by the Liberty Hotel to rent rooms and commemorate its disturbing history—but others believe the Nightmare on Charles Street festival is an attempt to embrace the frightening history of one of Boston's more disturbing reminders of how haunted Beantown really can be. Executions were carried out in the front yard starting in 1826. A sub-basement was rumored to be inhabited by multiple generations of feral cats and preternaturally-large rats.

Once considered an ideal prison, with many of its 282 granite cells having those views of the Charles River, the jail gradually fell into ruin, as penitentiaries often do. Its granite design construction was as innovative as how the jail was hidden from passing Bostonians by brick perimeter walls with barbed wire. The granite blocks, which came from nearby Quincy, were built into an octagonal center with four wings that radiated off from the center. High vaulted ceilings and large windows bathed the prisoners in natural daylight.

Over a hundred million dollars were spent purchasing, renovating and rebuilding the structure. Considering that notable crooks such as former Boston mayor James Michael Curley and confidence artist Frank Abagnale Junior have been held there—it is worth being mindful of the fact that the jail was closed for being too unsafe and unsanitary for prisoners. One cannot help but wonder if the Halloween revelers, in celebrating the haunted history of the Charles Street Jail, are aware of the dark forces that they might be conjuring. It can be presumed that far too few of the revelers realize that the hotel's bar is the area that was once the jail's drunk tank.

A scraggly tree is growing outside of what looks like the barred windows of a jail.

> ### The Liberty Hotel
> 215 Charles Street
> Boston MA
> 02144
> http://www.libertyhotel.com/

The Majestic Theater
(Cutler Majestic Theater at Emerson College)

The Majestic Theater is one of the oldest theaters in Boston. It opened on February 16th, 1903, and was commissioned by Eben Dyer Jordan, the son of the founder of the popular Jordan Marsh regional chain of department stores. At the time of its opening, 4,500 light bulbs, the popular new invention of the time, were installed in the lobby and auditorium. Architect John Galen Howard was local but had studied at the Beaux Arts School of Paris.

Classical architecture, including ionic columns on the outside, and modern decorative touches such as thick ornamental garlands of flowers and fruits combined to make it a distinctive building. The Majestic Theater began showing operas but, over the years, the theater was redesigned for vaudeville shows in the 1920s and then refurbished again when the theater began showing films. The Majestic was eventually renamed the Saxon Theater until that particular incarnation closed in 1983. A few years after the Saxon Theater stopped showing movies, Emerson College purchased the landmark and restored the theater to have live performances yet again.

At no point in its history has the Majestic Theater been free of spirits. A Boston mayor died during a show and is still seen sitting in his favorite seat. A little girl sneaks from aisle to aisle asking for presents and a married couple haunts the third floor balcony, sometimes dancing and other times wailing. Perhaps most feared of all is the "Nightmare

Room," a room where people are known to have trouble breathing, choking because of the smothering and claustrophobic energy that lurks there. All of these occurrences associated with the Majestic Theater are consistent and ongoing, demonstrating how the theater is closely tied to the overall history of hauntings in Boston.

Perhaps the most mysterious legend is the persistent belief that a mayor who was in office died at the Majestic and still comes to shows. While it is unclear who the mayor was, the best guess is George Albee Hibbard—a Republican who was mayor for only two years, from 1908 to 1910. Hibbard is the most likely ghostly suspect, in part because his wife took up performing after his death and made her debut at the Majestic. He may have been bothered that she played a cigarette-smoking showgirl who was obsessed with cars and diamonds.

Over the years, as the Majestic Theater opened and closed in its various forms, the building was sometimes left in a state of disrepair—but the theater has always found a way to come back to life. It is uncertain when these hauntings first began, partially because they have gone on for so long—but it is clear that the strange occurrences are continuing. Sometimes the little girl sneaking from aisle to aisle vanishes as soon as people see her, as if she has become more shy over time. The couple on the third floor balcony still wear their clothing from the Edwardian area and they are known to push down their favorite seats, leaving impressions on the fabric. For years, the third floor balcony was closed to the public to keep them from coming in contact with the spirits.

Now called the Cutler Majestic Theater at Emerson College, theater students working on performances have heard disconcerting and unexplained sounds, and have experienced inexplicable power failures. They report sensing unseen presences in the backstage area, the dressing rooms, and also in the sound room. It is often believed and repeated in Emerson lore that the spirits turn off the sound equipment for shows that the spirits do not particularly like. But the students who perform or work on the productions in the theater also tell stories that are focused on that third-floor balcony. Long ago, it was the only area in the theater where Boston's poorest and minority audiences could afford to sit. The third-floor balcony was steep and crowded with cramped seats. The balcony had been closed to the public for a long time, perhaps because for being a fire hazard, perhaps because it was haunted.

Yet the rational explanations cannot explain why the seats flip up and down. There is no rational explanation for why students have learned to say, "Excuse me," when they pass the seats that the dancing, Edwardian couple have lowered. It can only be because the students know that they are standing in the way of the ghosts' views of the stage. There have even been times when the seats have had weights laid upon them to keep the seats from loudly springing back up during performances.

Finally, after an extensive renovation that brought the theater back up to building codes, adding hand railings and other safety measures, including repairs to the fire exits, the Majestic's third-floor balcony was reopened. One can only hope that the ghosts do not rebel when all of these new and living theater-goers try to take their "reserved" seats or, worse, block their view of the stage.

Cutler Majestic Theater at Emerson College
219 Tremont Street
Boston, MA 02116-4717
To book a walking tour ($5.00 per person): (617) 824-8000
Monday-Saturday 10:00am-6:00pm (except holidays)
http://www.maj.org/

The Parker House Hotel
(The Omni Parker House)

In the heart of downtown, on the Freedom Trail and at the foot of Beacon Hill, the Parker House is the longest continuously operating high-end hotel in the entire United States. The Parker House opened in 1855 and would be highly regarded as an historic landmark even if the hotel were not also one of the most haunted hotels in the country.

Home of the Saturday Club that was founded by literary New Englanders such as Nathaniel Hawthorne, Henry Wadsworth Longfellow, Henry David Thoreau, and Ralph Waldo Emerson, the Parker House Hotel has also spawned the invention of cultural legends such as Boston cream pie, the tasty dinner roll known as the Parker House roll, and the phrase "scrod." Famed New Orleans chef and restaurateur Emeril Lagasse worked there. Even stranger, noted African-American activist Malcolm X was a busboy there in the 1940s and Vietnamese Communist revolutionary Ho Chi Minh baked in the hotel's bakeshop from 1911 to 1913. President John F. Kennedy announced that he was running for Congress from the Parker House Hotel and Kennedy also proposed to Jacqueline Bouvier and held his bachelor party there.

While ghostly sightings have been reported throughout the many floors of the building, the third floor and the elevators are considered the most particularly haunted spots. The famous actress of the 1800s, Charlotte Cushman, who played all of the major roles of the stage in her day—not just Lady Macbeth, but even Hamlet—died there in 1876. Now, one particular elevator goes by itself to the third floor even when no one has pressed a button.

The tenth floor has been known to fill with the sound of squeaking rocking chairs even though the hotel has checked everywhere and has been unable to find a single rocking chair, or anything that might make the sound, in the entire building. The tenth floor has had floating orbs of light that have been witnessed by several bellmen. The issues with the tenth floor seem connected with the hotel's founder, Harvey Parker.

Guests claiming encounters, over the years, with Harvey was probably less surprising before he died in 1884. Many guests state that Mr. Parker has approached them and asked for a detailed description of their stay and their experiences at his hotel. The elevators are also known to go to the tenth floor even when no buttons have been pushed, sometimes with Harvey Parker having been seen on board. Mr. Parker has most frequently been known to haunt his former hotel's tenth floor, but has been seen throughout the building and even out front.

In 1950, an elderly woman met Harvey outside of room 1078. He formed from thin air, starting as a dark mist, and then becoming more substantial. Harvey Parker turned to the elderly woman, now fully-formed as a large man with a mustache. The large mustached man vanished before her eyes.

The old woman went and got hotel security, but they could not find the former owner. In life and in death, Harvey Parker is obviously known to be a detail-oriented and hands-on owner. Whether it was the famous literary figures of the Saturday Club, or less famous guests, Harvey Parker always wanted to make sure that they enjoyed every aspect of their stay… which is probably why he never left.

Among the hotels across the country that are known to be haunted, the Parker House, now officially called the Omni Parker House, is one of the best known for having had its patrons visited by the long-dead former proprietor. One cannot help find a way to respect a proprietor who pays so much attention to detail that he checks up on guests long after his demise. Mr. Parker's approach to customer service sounds terrifying, but it also shows him to be very conscientious.

Omni Parker House
60 School Street
Boston, Massachusetts 02108
Phone: (617) 227-8600
Fax: (617) 742-5729
http://www.omnihotels.com/FindAHotel/BostonParkerHouse.aspx

The Curse of the Bambino

In 1903, the Boston Red Sox won the first World Series, and then quickly won four more, wining five championships in the first fifteen years of the existence of the World Series. In 1918, Babe Ruth, "The Bambino," led the team to the World Series over the Chicago Cubs. Then in 1920, Ruth was sold to the New York Yankees. Ruth had done well for the Red Sox, even setting a record that still stands today by pitching thirteen scoreless innings during the 1916 World Series, but he was not long for Boston. The Boston Red Sox would not win another World Series for eighty-six years. Generations of fans were born, grew old, and even died without ever seeing their favorite team with another championship. As Rand Richards Cooper wrote in the *Culture Journal Commonwealth* just months before the curse was finally broken, "By now Red Sox suffering surpasses an individual human life span. It is a cathedral of loss and pain. It is holy."

Meanwhile, the New York Yankees, a team that had never made it to the World Series prior to 1918, built a stunning dynasty. Not only did Babe Ruth become one of the greatest baseball players of all time, the Yankees became the "winningest" team in Major League Baseball, with twenty-six World Series wins and thirty-nine American League pennants. The Red Sox made it to the World Series only four times prior to 2004, and each time dropped the seventh game to return home as losers.

In 1986, the Red Sox collapsed against the New York Mets in the sixth and seventh games of the World Series, giving up a 3-0 lead to lose 8-5 in the final game. *New York Times* sportswriter George Vecsey jokingly referred to "Babe Ruth's Curse" in analyzing these two games, and a legend was born. The idea of a curse took off, leading to a number of comical attempts to break the spell—a Red Sox cap was left at the peaks of Mount Everest, and a "Reverse Curve" street sign in Boston was vandalized to read "Reverse the Curse." Of course, New York fans tried to augment the curse, even chanting "1918! 1918!" when the Sox played Yankee Stadium.

Is the "curse of the Bambino" really all that creepy? The Chicago Cubs have their own "curse of the billy goat," the fallout of which even involved a butchered goat being hung from the statue of Harry Caray in 2007. The Red Sox curse seemed downright quaint, just one more element of the largely one-sided rivalry between Boston and New York City, with Boston ever being a "second city" to Gotham. But Boston is perhaps the greatest sports town in the United States. Major national chains such as Barnes & Noble, for example, bar their employees from wearing clothes with logos and corporate symbols, except in Boston, where Red Sox gear is allowed for the simple reason that otherwise customers would feel uncomfortable during baseball season. Red Sox fans see Fenway Park as a cathedral, even going so far as to, in 1983, gather atop the famed CITGO sign that decorates the park like a jewel in a crown. Sox fans had the sign declared a landmark, and Marty Foley, the man in charge of maintaining the sign and its many LEDs, has been given the mystical-sounding name Keeper of the Sign.

The great slugger Babe Ruth even has his own postage stamp.

The Red Sox Nation, after its long drought, can never be satisfied with World Series wins. The curse is broken, but the wounds may never heal. The curse brought Boston together, and changed life in the city utterly.

In 2004, the Red Sox made it to the American League Championship Series and faced the New York Yankees. New York City and Boston are just a few hours drive apart, and a largely one-sided rivalry had been heating up since the "curse" was discovered. Red Sox fans are said to have two favorite teams: the Sox and whoever can beat the Yankees. The Series did not go well for the Sox at first, as the team lost the first three games. A stunning comeback at the bottom of the ninth inning in game four gave Boston some breathing room, and the team won the next three games as well, moving on to the World Series. There, the team faced the St. Louis Cardinals, which had beaten the Sox in the Series in 1946 and 1967. This time, it wasn't even close. The Sox swept the Series, and finally the "curse of The Bambino" was broken. We know for sure that the curse has been destroyed because the Sox also won the 2007 World Series, destroying the Colorado Rockies in four games. On Downtown Crossing, in Harvard Square, as far north as Brattleboro, Vermont, and as far south as Hartford Connecticut, a million Red Sox logos bloom, a million blood-red talismans hold off the return of the curse. If you're a baseball fan, the curse is one more thing to struggle with, but if you are ever in Boston and make the error of not following the nation's pastime, or worse, rooting for the Yankees, you'll learn how creepy Boston can be.

Fenway Park
4 Yawkey Way,
Boston, MA 02215
http://boston.redsox.mlb.com

The Isabella Stewart Gardner Museum

Small art museums aren't necessarily all spooky or creepy, generally speaking. And indeed for much of its life the Isabella Stewart Gardner Museum was neither. Founded in 1896 by the pepper fortune heiress (yes, pepper was a big import) it opened in 1903 in a custom-built palazzo influenced heavily by Gardner's own tastes. Gardner's tastes were unusual: she posed nude for guests at parties, and walked lions down the streets of Boston. Some claim she was the model for Isabel Archer, the immortal lady in the Henry James novel *Portrait of a Lady*. The museum was as innovative as Gardner herself at the time of its founding; its glass-roofed courtyard was the first in the United States. The museum's collection is idiosyncratic and also includes a musical performance series, the longest-running in the United States. Tapestries, Japanese screens, rare books, American artists such as Singer (who painted a portrait of Isabella Gardner), jewelry, and Italian Renaissance painting. And also some empty frames. And this is where things start getting creepy… Douglass Shand-Tucci, Gardner's biographer, claimed that due to the theft, the museum itself is now "touched with evil…in a way that has deepened the experience" of visiting it.

In the early morning hours of March 18, 1990, two thieves in police uniforms ignored the nearby Museum of Fine Arts to enter the Fenway-Kenmore neighborhood's more accessible museum. They claimed to be investigating a disturbance, and then caused one. The criminals handcuffed the security guards and made off with thirteen paintings including originals by Rembrandt, Manet, five by Degas, and *The Concert* by Vermeer, which is now considered the world's most popular stolen painting. This theft is valued at over half a *billion* dollars, making it the greatest single theft of private property in the history of the world, and certainly the greatest and most audacious art theft. Due to a codicil in Gardner's will, the museum's collection cannot be changed. Nothing may be added to it, and nothing taken away. Thus empty frames have been on the walls where such paintings as Vermeer's *The Concert*, and Rembrandt's only seascape, *The Storm on the Sea of Galilee* were once displayed. That's only mildly creepy though.

The thefts remain unsolved to this day, despite immense manpower and a five million dollar reward for information leading to the recovery of the paintings. Some observers have suspected James J. "Whitey" Bulger, erstwhile leader of the Winter Hill Gang and FBI Most Wanted perennial. Were the paintings sold to millionaire collectors and the money sent to the Irish Republican Army for arms? Perhaps such a claim is far-fetched, but the IRA has engaged in art thefts in the past, and seem to have "a thing" for Vermeers, according to author and Vermeer scholar Katharine Weber. IRA members have stolen Vermeer works in the past, including *Lady Writing a Letter with her Maid* in a daring 1974 raid on the famed Russborough House in County Wicklow, Ireland. However, there is no definitive evidence tying the Gardner paintings to the IRA. Are they actually still in Boston, as some have claimed?

Until his death in 2005, famed art detective Harold Smith was on the case. A figure who seemingly sprung from the pages of pulp fiction, Smith dressed impeccably in a bowler hat and cane, but his wardrobe was the least of his peculiarities. While a sailor, Smith contracted a skin condition and allowed himself to be exposed to radiation in an experimental attempt to treat it. Instead, Smith lost his nose, an eye, and a lung to cancer. With an eye patch and an unusual-looking false nose, Smith wasn't much for undercover work, but his success with other art cases spoke for itself. Sadly, he succumbed to his disease before cracking this case. The paintings are still out there somewhere, and the reward still set. Gardner specialists have said that if she was still alive, she would have reclaimed the paintings by now—a hint at some of the untoward maneuvers she used to complete her collection.

The Gardner Museum is unique—it's the only museum in the world designed by a woman, with a collection chosen by a woman, and perhaps still inhabited by a woman. Long before the thefts, Gardner claimed someone else in spirit. Long-time gallery attendant Frank DiMaria has worked at the museum for over forty years and dedicated his life to the long-dead millionaires after visiting the museum as a child. There, at age thirteen, he stood before the imposing portrait painted by John Singer Sargent and heard Gardner's voice say to him, "You're mine, and you'll know me all your life." No others have claimed so publicly to have heard from Gardner, but perhaps you'll be next…

The museum and theft were featured in the documentary film *Stolen* and also in the book *The Gardner Heist* by Ulrich Boser, whose work is based partially on files he inherited from Harold Smith. *Stolen* received a theatrical release and has also been aired on cable. It is available for viewing for free and in its entirety online: http://www.snagfilms.com/films/title/stolen/ at this writing.

> ## Isabella Stewart Gardner Museum
> 280 The Fenway, Boston MA 02115
> Information: (617) 566-1401
> Box Office: (617) 278-5156

Margery versus Houdini

Boston was the home of the Puritans, who despised the very notion of witchcraft or magic. Of course they believed such things to be real— it was the idea of trafficking with Satan in violation of God's law that drove the fascination with the supernatural among Bostonians (and Salemites!). Puritanism fell into decline but the attraction to the Other World remained well into the twentieth century. The Spiritualist movement in the United States prospered in Boston, and met its match there in the figure of Harry Houdini.

The stage magician and escape artist was himself endlessly attracted to the idea of the supernatural—and this thanks partially to his friendship with Arthur Conan Doyle, the credulous author of the Sherlock Holmes mysteries—but his knowledge of prestidigitation and stage effects quickly disabused him of any belief he may have had in spirit mediums, séances, and communication after death. Houdini was a member of the *avant garde* as far as skepticism went. Though the Spiritualist movement was in decline by the 1920s, a near-universal belief in the soul combined with the wildness of the "Roaring Twenties" led to a questioning of the religious status quo. Mediums were back, and science was in vogue. The magazine *Scientific American* even offered a $2500 bounty for proof of "conclusive psychic manifestations" under controlled conditions. And the leading contender was Boston's Mina Crandon, who in 1924 was a thirty-six-year-old doctor's wife also known as "Margery."

Margery was the toast of Boston. With her husband Dr. Le Roi Goddard Crandon, a surgeon and instructor at Harvard Medical School, she lived in Tony Beacon Hill on 11 Lime Street, and there rubbed shoulders with the Boston Brahmins and the rest of the city's elite. The Crandons certainly weren't in a position where it would have made sense to engage in a scam for a mere twenty-five hundred dollars, and indeed in the beginning did little more than put on séances for their friends. Harvard psychologist William McDougall sat with Margery at several invitation-only sessions and was somewhat impressed. Though he believed that many of the "telekinesis" effects Margery demonstrated were fraudulent, he was unsure as to her claims of spirit mediumship and communication with forces from beyond the grave. McDougall was also part of the *Scientific American* investigation team, so perhaps this is why the Crandons took a chance with a jury of scientists and the famed Houdini. They did decide to call Mina "Margery" for the media though, to keep his wife's claims (and perhaps his own) from negatively impacting his career and social status.

Today, Margery's tricks sound basic enough. She would ring an electric bell under the table, supposedly without the use of her hands or feet. Margery's claim was that the spirit of her late brother, Walter, was ringing the bell on her command. She also produced gloves and even wax impressions of fingerprints from the dead, "materialized" a number of other objects, and spoke in trance in many voices and even different languages. However, in the modern era, no group of judges from a major scientific journal would allow a so-called medium to supply her own electric bell, nor would they allow it to be obscured by a table. Margery went so far as to tell the judges, "Just press hard against my ankle so that you can see that my ankle is there."

But scientists are not magicians, or as Houdini himself said, "It takes a flimflammer to catch a flimflammer." The magician had bound his own leg very tightly, and then released the binding right before the beginning of the séance, so that his leg would be very sensitive to even the slightest of movements. He felt her leg move to put pressure on the board covering the bell, which would cause it to ring.

Other manifestations could also be duplicated. A glowing rod of "ectoplasm" could have been a knitting needle moved about in the dark of the room by Margery using her mouth. The phantom megaphone that appeared before Houdini was probably simply balanced first on the edge of the cabinet in which she did her work, and then when she kicked the cabinet over it landed on the psychic's head in the manner of a dunce cap. From there, she need only toss her head to "produce" the horn. Houdini, in his pamphlet *"Margery" the Medium Exposed* called this "the 'slickest' ruse I have ever detected, and it has converted all skeptics."

There were other slick moves as well. A folding ruler was found at Margery's feet after one séance, and an eraser had been placed under the bell, perhaps to keep it from ringing, after another event. While to a disinterested skeptic it would be clear that Margery used these devices to create her effects, other committee members claimed that Houdini had planted the materials himself in order to discredit Margery. Houdini himself saw this as a double-play: the clever Margery "sloppily" allowed her ruler to be viewed so that Houdini himself could be discredited.

And indeed, the conflict between the skeptic and the "open-minded" scientists was a problem—when Houdini was away it was leaked to the press that the other members of the *Scientific American* committee were about to vote in favor of Margery. Houdini quickly released the pamphlet to counter such a disaster and gave a performance at Symphony Hall in January of 2005, where he demonstrated many of Margery's tricks. Margery launched her own performance a few days later at Jordan Hall, and then refused any further testing. Only then did the committee vote against awarding Mina Crandon the prize.

Margery's career did not end with Houdini's revelations. And indeed, here is where the story gets truly creepy. "Walter" in one of the final encounters with Houdini, placed a curse on the magician and declared that Houdini would be dead within a year. And just over a year later, Houdini was killed by a punch to the stomach…the sort of blow that had led some to wonder if Houdini was actually poisoned by supporters of the Spiritualist movement. After all, spirit mediums often preyed on the wealthy elderly, especially those with few relatives, a habit of changing their wills, and who need only a little bit of poison "help" to enter the great beyond themselves. Was poison a fundamental part of the Spiritualist scam, and if so did Houdini fall prey to his enemies? The authors of the 2007 biography *The Secret Life of Houdini* even attempted to have the magician's body exhumed to determine if poison had killed Houdini… and of course to get the name of their book in the newspapers.

And after Houdini shuffled off this mortal coil, Margery continued her act for Boston's elite and the occasional researcher, this time "manifesting" physical "teleplasm" that looked like the dead hands of the spirits. These "hands" were real, and could be touched and manipulated by observers, but they were never surrendered after the séances. What could they have been? Some sources suggest that they were crudely carved pieces of lung tissue, which could have easily been created by Dr. Crandon. Or, as some claim, they could have actually been a part of Margery's body—did the wealthy Harvard surgeon actually carve his wife's genitals into an abnormal "hand" to be presented to the credulous and curious in the middle of his darkened living room? If so, perhaps such a kinky display was the ultimate reason why the Crandon's submitted to continued voyeuristic demonstrations.

In the end, Margery had a few believers including Arthur Conan Doyle, who once purchased ads in Boston newspapers that read simply "J. B. Rhine is an ass" in support of his favorite medium. (Rhine, the paranormal researcher after whom the famous testing cards used in telepathy experiments is named, was not impressed with Margery's tricks.) Margery finally fell out of the public limelight when one last trick was revealed—"Walter" would often leave fingerprints from beyond the grave in a bit of wax, but the fingerprints and the wax were both revealed as having come from Margery's dentist. After Dr. Crandon's death, Margery turned to alcohol and once nearly flung herself from the roof of her Lime Street home. She died in 1941, even as her few supporters demanded ever more demonstrations of her psychic prowess. Since her death though, we haven't heard from her...

Poe's Boston

The thousand injuries of Fortunato I had borne as I best could; but when he ventured upon insult, I vowed revenge. You, who so well know the nature of my soul, will not suppose, however, that I gave utterance to a threat. At length I would be avenged; this was a point definitively settled—but the very definitiveness with which it was resolved, precluded the idea of risk.

—Edgar Allan Poe
"The Cask of Amontillado"

Edgar Allan Poe, America's greatest writer of dark fiction and poetry, was born in Boston. His first book, a thin volume called *Tamerlane and Other Poems,* he self-published—as was done at the time since there was little in the way of an American publishing industry to speak of—was credited simply to "a Bostonian" in 1827. As a young soldier, he was stationed at nearby Fort Independence on Castle Island. In later years though, Poe grew to despise Boston and many of its famous writers, such as Thoreau and Longfellow. Feeling marginalized by the city, which had become a center of publishing, and by the intelligentsia which wanted little to do with Poe's macabre visions, Poe spent much of his life elsewhere—New York, Philadelphia, Richmond, and most famously Baltimore. From afar, he fired literary arrows at the great city, at one point proclaiming, "Their hotels are bad. Their pumpkin pies are delicious. Their poetry is not so good." He disliked the Transcendentalists for what he saw as their mysticism and willful obscurity, referring to them as "Frogpondians," a term which not only refers to the empty ribbits of Thoreau et al, but which is also an insult aimed at the Boston Common and its pond. Of the residents of the city, he simply said, "Bostonians have no soul. ...The Bostonians are well-bred–as very dull persons very generally are."

Toward the end of his life though, Poe made public a wish to be buried in Boston. And it was a peculiar Boston burial that helped make Poe one of the greatest writers of all time. Fort Independence on Castle Island is one of the oldest forts in North America. Built in 1643 in Fort William and Mary by the British, it gained its new name in 1779, and played an important role in the defense of Boston during the War of 1812. The fort was nearly 200 years old by the time Poe took his station there with Battery H of the First Artillery in 1827, the same year he published his first slim volume of poems in an edition of fifty copies. Penniless, without any skill save writing, and rather bored as soldiers are, Poe took an interest in one of the local legends. There was a monument in the fort at the time to Lieutenant Robert Massie, who died ten years prior in a duel with Lieutenant Gustavis Drane on Christmas Day. Massie was popular on the base, and Drane much less so. And that was before the duel and his murder of Massie. Other soldiers, it was said, got their revenge by getting Drane drunk later that night and then leading him down to the dungeon in the bowels of the fort. There Drane, inebriated to the brink of unconsciousness, was walled in to a vault.

If it sounds familiar, it should be. That is, in essence, the plot to "The Cask of Amontillado," published in 1846. "Cask" was one of Poe's later stories, published a year after his great success with "The Raven" and also after a lengthy literary feud with both the Transcendentalists and the poet Henry Wadsworth Longfellow, whom he had accused of plagiarism. Poe was never satisfied with his own successes though, and hungered for the chance to conquer and humiliate the writers he saw as rivals. Did Poe reach back to the lowest part of his life and transform himself into a hero at the time when his fortunes were at their peak? He was the vicious Montresor, whom no one could attack with impunity, and who was his great rival but the aptly named Fortunato, a symbol of all

Poe's literary competition (and what he saw as their unearned success). Poe's star began to fall soon after though, and by 1848 he was back in Boston, where he attempted suicide via an opiate overdose. His wish to be buried in Boston did not come true however; after surviving that suicide attempt, Poe made his way back to Baltimore where he died under mysterious circumstances less than a year later.

There are literary antecedents to "The Cask of Amontillado." Some Poe scholars point to the Boston-area Castle Island story and to rumors of the skeleton reported found in the subterranean areas of Fort Independence, while others note that Joel Headley's "A Man Built in a Wall" was published two years prior to Poe's story, and has a similar plot and an Italian setting. Bostonians have happily recited the Castle Island story for generations, in an attempt to reclaim their darkest favorite son for the Athens of America. And the alternative…that Poe himself was a plagiarist, might be too terrible to bear.

Poe was born in 1809 yards from Boston Common, which he denounced as nothing more than a frog pond. In 2009, in celebration of his bicentennial, the corner of Boylston and Charles Streets, right off the Common, was renamed Poe Square. Poe wished to have been buried in Boston, but also suffered from a life-long phobia of being buried alive. It's a good thing that his body is far from Boston Common then, as the sound of the frogs in the ponds by the patch of land that brought him into this world and bears his name would likely drive him mad.

Castle Island has fared a bit better. Now open to the public and administered by the all-volunteer Castle Island Association, there are free tours of island and fort in the afternoons of the summer and autumn months, weather permitting. Perhaps as a nod to Poe's own inspirations, one of the largest events on the island is the annual Children's Magical Halloween Castle, which is held on the fourth weekend of October and attracts thousands.

Fort Independence and Castle Island
Castle Island Association, P. O. Box 342,
South Boston, MA 02127
(617) 268-8870
http://www.bostonfortindependence.com/

Edgar Allan Poe Square
(Note: little is here for Poe fans save a plaque,
but the location is adjacent to
Boston Common and Downtown Crossing)
Boylston St & Charles St. S, Boston, MA 02116

Chapter Three
Colleges

Harvard Haunting and Others

Boston is America's greatest college town. Between Boston and its immediate suburbs, there are over fifty colleges and universities, including some of the largest (Boston University), and most prestigious (Harvard and the Massachusetts Institute of Technology, on opposite ends of Cambridge), and innovative (Lesley). The oldest of these schools predate the founding of the United States of America itself, and so ghost stories abound.

Boston-area colleges are not only often ancient, but have cultures of their own. The passing down of legends and stories is one way in which colleges create their own legacies and reputations. For every press release about this or that achievement, though, there is an underground tale passed on from clever upper classman to credulous freshmen who have never before left home.

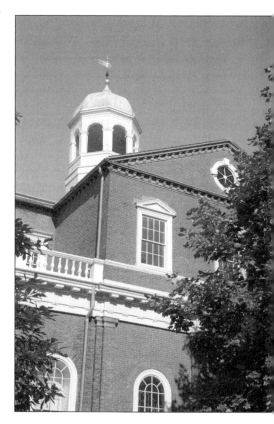

Here, in this sunny day photograph from Harvard campus, no ghosts are visible, but the legends of students say otherwise.

Nothing makes the first night in a strange dorm more forlorn or creepy than tales that explain every groan of the pipes, malfunctioning heating system, or distant yelp from a suitemate in the midst of an anxiety dream.

Harvard University, for example, is where the ruling class of the United States is trained. Yet its local legend is rather more proletarian: Thayer Hall was supposedly home to a textile mill in the nineteenth century. Now one of the largest of Harvard's freshman dormitories, Thayer Hall does indeed look like one of the many red brick factory buildings that fueled the economy of much of New England for more than a century. There have been reports of students seeing apparitions clad in "Victorian" clothing for years, and it is said that these ghosts go about their daily business at night according to floorplans that no longer correspond to the many individual rooms that comprise the building. *Harvard Crimson* in 2009 asked, Josh A. Bookin, a Thayer proctor, if he had seen anything after a reporter heard of the haunting on a website, but Bookin simply remarked, "I have seen no evidence to that so far."

In the business of ghost hunting and folklore, it is easy enough for a legend to be created, whole cloth, from anyone with a website and a bit of imagination, but as far as the Thayer ghosts go, noted folklorist Joseph A. Citro has also made mention of these sightings several years before. Perhaps there is just a ghost of guilt—the world's wealthiest teens and young adults live in Thayer Hall; perhaps they should be haunted by the ghosts of laborers who may well have worked themselves to death. Further, Citro also claims that assistant dean of freshmen William C. Young once encountered a ghost in Massachusetts Hall, another of the freshman dorms and, built in 1718, the oldest building in Harvard Square. Who that ghost may be remains undetermined, but given that the building is nearly 300 years old, there are many, many possible candidates.

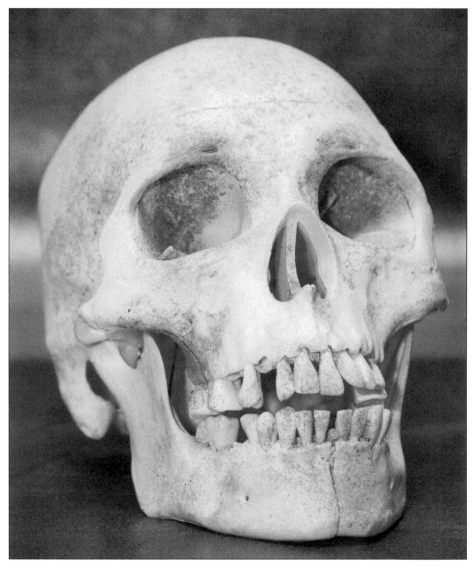

Across the country, colleges and universities are known
for stories where founders' skulls are stolen.

The newer colleges have more modern ghosts. Students have been reporting that Boston University's Shelton Hall is haunted for decades. A mix of poltergeist-type effects are common: scratching and strange sounds, lights dimming, elevator doors that open without being called, and, "[l]ights flickering, or strange sounds in the corridor. Knock on the door, and when they would open the door there would be nothing there," David Zamojski told local radio station WBUR in late 2009. Zamojski lived in Shelton Hall in the 1980s and is now the director of residence life at Boston University. His recollections match the current experiences of students, who report their strange experiences on a bulletin board in the dorm.

Intriguingly, the ghost is widely believed to be that of the famed playwright Eugene O' Neill. In the 1950s, Shelton Hall was Shelton Hotel—one of the first of the Sheraton chain—and O'Neill spent his last days there, tortured by Parkinson's Disease, alcoholism, and his own inability to write. O'Neill is buried nearby at Boston's Forest Hills Cemetery. No word yet on whether he helps Shelton Hall students with their term papers on *Long Day's Journey Into Night.*

Boston College, a Catholic school, has few ghost stories. Indeed, in the earlier part of this decade, the independent student newspaper *The Heights* went looking for ghost stories and came up empty-handed, or nearly so. Despite, or perhaps because of, the school's Gothic architecture and Roman Catholic tradition, students, faculty, and alumni were tightlipped about any so-called supernatural events on campus. Then, after the first newspaper story was published on the failure to find any ghost stories, former managers and residents of the school's O'Connell House, which now houses the student union, stepped forward.

The mansion was once known as the Liggett family estate, and it is claimed that either the family patriarch killed his wife's lover, who still haunts the house, or a Liggett uncle may have killed his niece in a crime of passion, and some believe that she is an active ghost. "I am sure you have heard the stories about the woman who used to be locked up in one section of the house and hates keys and locked things. As I recall, she is bound to the house until someone can solve or more fully explain a death that took place in the house which she apparently thinks was covered up," building manager Patrick Moran wrote in 1997. This ghost is well known for opening doors and windows, them slamming them shut. She has even managed to open and them slam shut windows in the building's attic—despite the fact that the original windows were replaced with single-pane glass that cannot be opened.

There are also tales of a five-year-old boy who drowned in the pool that used to be part of the building, and even stories of a ghost dog. Feven Teklu, a BC student, told the *Chronicle*, BC's faculty and staff newspaper in 2002, "every now and then I'll be lying in bed and see this little dog sitting under my desk looking at me...It's there and then it disappears. It's kind of eerie and definitely a mystery."

Of course, given the creaky, aging buildings and the tendency for college students to stay up all night—to study, surely—it is not unusual that the colleges of Boston have their fair share of chilling stories to be passed from generation to generation. Harvard even looks a bit like Hogwarts...though the ghosts are, thankfully, a bit less chatty.

Note: these dormitories and student buildings are generally not open to the public.

Sometimes when students stay up all night, they may even see things that are not there. *Photo courtesy of Jayna Lloyd of Jayna Sullivan Photography.*

Harvard University

Cambridge, MA 02138

Tel: (617) 495-1000

Fax: (617) 495-0754

http://www.hcs.harvard.edu/~dorms/

Shelton Hall

Boston University

91 Bay State Road

Boston, MA 02215

(617) 353-3852

http://www.bu.edu/housing/residences/largedorms/shelton.html

The O'Connell House Student Union

Boston College

140 Commonwealth Ave

Chestnut Hill, Massachusetts 02167

(617) 552-4310

http://www.bc.edu/bc_org/svp/st_org/ochouse/default.html

Chapter Four

Chappaquiddick Island

Chappaquiddick Island is today known for virtually one tragic event—the death of Mary Jo Kopechne, who drowned in a car belonging to Senator Edward Kennedy in the early morning hours of July 19, 1969. Kennedy had made a wrong turn and plunged his car into Pucha Pond. The Senator was able to swim free of the car, but Kopechne was not. Kennedy did not report the accident or Kopechne's fate to the police, and she was found the next morning by fisherman. Of course a public scandal ensued—why was the married Kennedy driving off with someone other than his wife? Was he inebriated? Why didn't he depend on his chauffeur that evening? Why didn't he report the incident to the police immediately? Kennedy, with the popular support of a majority of Massachusetts voters, did not resign his seat and received a suspended sentence and had his driver's license suspended for six months after pleading guilty to leaving the scene of an accident after causing injury. Kennedy held his Senate seat until his death in 2009, after being elected nine times and serving the third-longest term in the history of the Senate. Chappaquiddick dogged Kennedy though, and almost surely kept him from running for the Oval Office in 1972, or winning the Democratic Party nomination in 1980.

The long shadow of the Kennedy family extends over all of Massachusetts, but on Chappaquiddick Island the shadow is likely the darkest. It's a sad irony too, for that all-American family's influence on the popular understanding of the island obscures an almost non-American history. The tiny island, which until 2007 was connected by Katama Beach to Martha's Vineyard, is one of the very tips of the nation. Well into the

1820s, the small island was dominated by the Wampanoag Indians despite a settler presence there since the 1640s and the devastation of King Philip's War in 1676. A reservation remains on the island today. The few locals—fewer than 200 people live on the small island today—call the brief trip to Martha's Vineyard "going to the mainland" and refer to trips to the rest of the state as "going to America." This unique island is also haunted.

Ben C. Clough, writing for the *Journal of American Folklore* in 1918 discusses two legends of the area, which he calls the Haunted Hollow and the Little Man. The Haunted Hollow is a very traditional "warning" story to young mothers—in the early 1800s, a woman of questionable character lived on the island with her several children. She would lock them in the house at night and take the late ferry, then likely little more than a rowboat, to Edgartown on Martha's Vineyard. What a single woman with several children might be doing late at night on Martha's Vineyard was left to the lurid imagination of the early twentieth-century reader, but surely no good would come of it. And indeed, the children managed to set a fire in their little home one night and were unable to escape being locked in and were burnt to death. In the haunted hollow, on certain nights, one is said to be able to hear the screaming and crying of three young children begging for their mother to come and save them, but of course she never does.

Clough's second legend is a bit more whimsical. The Little Man is a funny-looking little fellow, very short and certainly not known to anyone on the island. Very peculiar, of course, since it was and still is nearly impossible to live on Chappaquiddick and not know every other resident by sight. The little man would never say anything when he encountered a person, but simply point out toward the sea. Those meeting the Little Man would naturally (or perhaps supernaturally) feel compelled to turn in the direction the man pointed and when they would turn back around, he would have vanished. This legend is likely a survival of myths of the wee people and fairies brought over from the British isles and indeed Clough himself suggests that the figure is from a Scottish ballad in which someone is "walking all alone/Between a water and a wa" only to encounter a "wee wee man" who "in a twinkling of an eye…was clean awa."

The "warning" story and a the story of a little person are common enough ghost stories, and even an island as small as Chappaquiddick is destined to have something going on. One cannot help but connect some dots though, between the lost children of Haunted Hollow and poor Mary Jo Kopechne, also abandoned to die. But in water instead of fire? Well, what was the Little Man there to point to, if not perhaps the spot which decades later would make a watery grave for a young girl?

Lizzie Borden

Bridget Sullivan

Chapter Five

Lizzie Borden

"Lizzie Borden took an axe
And gave her mother forty whacks.
When she saw what she had done
She gave her father forty-one."

(a popular song sung while jumping rope)

About an hour-long drive south of Boston is the infamous town of Fall River. There, on Thursday, August 4th, 1892, a thirty-two-year-old woman made history by allegedly murdering her father and stepmother in particularly bloodthirsty ways. The murders, trial, and the media coverage made history in a way that few other crimes in American history ever have. She was acquitted, but Lizzie Borden is considered one of the most gruesome murderers the country has ever known.

Andrew Jackson Borden, her father, and Abby Durfee Borden, her stepmother, were both smashed with an ax, over and over, in the family home. Andrew suffered at least eleven blows to the head before the killer finally stopped swinging. For Abby, it was nineteen times. Lizzie Borden and the family's maid Bridget Sullivan were the only people in the residence and police quickly focused in on Lizzie as the only possible suspect. Bridget Sullivan was ruled out in part because Lizzie's behavior was considered suspect and in part because Bridget Sullivan provided important witness testimony for the inquest, preliminary hearing, and the final trial. Emma Lenora Borden, Lizzie Borden's sister, was away from the home at the time.

Andrew Borden had run errands that morning. He went to the bank and the Post Office and then returned home around 10:45AM. Lizzie reported stumbling over his dead body about half an hour later. Bridget Sullivan, the housekeeper, stated that she had been resting in her room on the third floor when she heard Lizzie screaming that someone had killed her father. Andrew Borden was on a couch in the sitting room on the first floor. He had been struck so hard that his skull was crushed and his left eyeball had been split open.

Neighbors and the family doctor were called immediately. While the neighbors and physicians were comforting Lizzie, Bridget Sullivan found the body of Abby Borden in a guest bedroom upstairs. Abby Borden had also been dispatched by bloody and violent whacks to the head.

On August 11th, 1892, Lizzie Borden was officially arrested for the crime. She had been previously questioned by the police, but the deciding factor had been that, on August 7th, a witness stated that Lizzie had burned a stained blue dress in the home's kitchen stove. On December 2nd, Lizzie was formally charged and the trial began ten months later, on June 5th, 1893, in New Bedford, Massachusetts. After a fourteen-day trial, the jury found her innocent of all charges, making their decision after deliberating for a little over an hour.

The police had discovered a hatchet in the Borden home's basement, but the hatchet was clean and was considered unlikely to be the murder weapon by most of the detectives, though some believed that the specific hatchet was the actual murder weapon.

One of the mysteries is how any killer could have made it up and down the stairs so quickly without leaving a trial of blood.
Photo courtesy of Renee Des Anges.

Some contemporary researchers believe Lizzie's prosecution would have been more effective if fingerprinting—a new and not fully understood technology at the time—had been put to use at the time of the trial. Lizzie had managed to explain away burning the blue dress in the kitchen stove by saying that she had accidentally smeared fresh paint on it. The primary reason that Lizzie was found not guilty was that there was no weapon and no blood evidence, leading to the jury finding there to be reasonable doubt. It seems that the jury could not figure out how she had cleaned up so quickly after two bloody murders.

Another theory is that a passing murderer managed to sneak through town without being noticed.

After the trial, Lizzie and her sister Emma, who had also lived in the home but had not been present on the day of the murders, purchased a thirteen-room house together and named their new residence Maplecroft, even having the name carved into the front step. The Borden sisters lived on the money they had inherited from the death of their parents until a quarrel in 1905 led to a serious falling out between the two of them. Some believe that the estrangement was motivated by Lizzie's strangely intimate relationship with a popular actress named Nance O'Neil. Of course, Lizzie's notoriety followed her for the rest of her life.

Borden eventually died in Fall River on June 1st of 1927, and was buried in Oak Grove Cemetery under the name of Lizbeth Andrew Borden. In her will, Lizzie Borden left a large sum to a local animal rescue league and also gave money to establish perpetual tending of her father's grave. Nine days later, Emma died from a sudden and unexpected fall in Newmarket, New Hampshire, where she had relocated after her estrangement from Lizzie. Nance O'Neil eventually capitalized on her relationship with Lizzie by appearing in a musical inspired by her famous friend.

For the contemporary Borden aficionado, the house where the murders occurred is now a bed and breakfast and also a museum. Visitors can lie their weary bones down on the sofa where Andrew Borden died or visitors can sleep in the very room where Abby Borden was killed. As would be expected, there are reports that a woman can be heard to cry out or scream, doors are said to slam for no reason, and footsteps are often heard running up and down the stairs.

What is known for certain is that the murders were never actually solved. Lizzie's defense lawyers have still not released their notes and records from over a century ago and theories are still rampant. Proponents of one of the prominent theories contend that Lizzie had knowledge of the murders and tend to focus on her being the one who committed the axe murders, often in collusion with the housekeeper, Bridget Sullivan, her sister Emma or even a deranged half-brother who may or may not have really existed. Lizzie remains the likely murderer despite her being found innocent in a court of law. An anonymous intruder makes for a wonderful explanation of how there was so little evidence (such as a weapon) at the scene, but the intruder idea seems unbelievable because a person running down the street covered in blood would surely be noticed. Even daydreamers notice people covered in blood who are running down the street.

The primary issue with the case is that so little is certain. Lizzie was found not guilty, at least to some degree, because she lived in an era when women were not seen as likely to murder. There are allegations that, as with Nance O'Neil, Lizzie had a romantic relationship with Bridget Sullivan. As witnesses, Bridget Sullivan and Lizzie Borden contradicted the testimony of the other and sometimes even contradicted their own testimony. The murder weapon was never found. Somehow someone disappeared who would have had to have been coated in blood. If there had not been the two corpses themselves, there would have been no evidence that the murder actually occurred. The reason that most believe Lizzie killed her parents is that she was the most likely to have a motive (ranging from loathing her parents to financial gain) and because of the dress that she burned.

Lizzie Borden Bed & Breakfast
92 Second Street, Fall River, MA 02721
Telephone 508-675-7333
Fax 508-673-1545
info@lizzie-borden.com

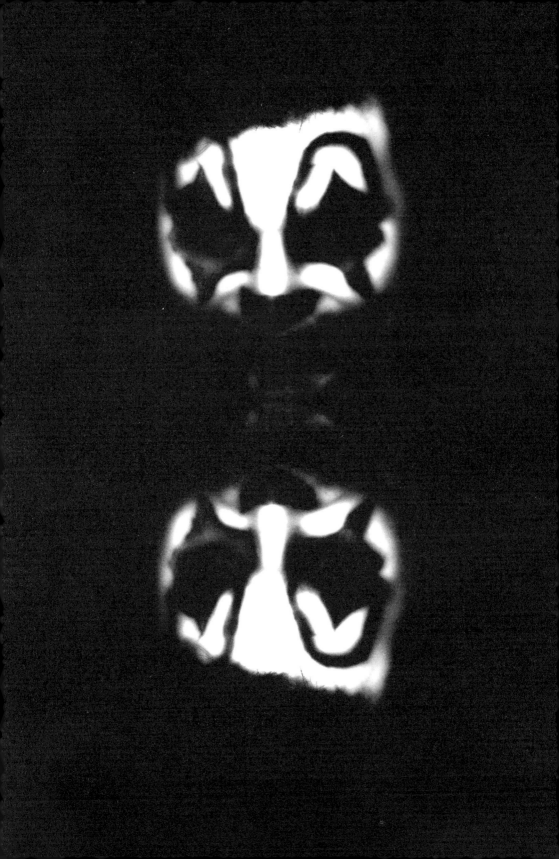

Chapter Six
Hospitals and Asylums

"Jolly" Jane Toppan

"I have an uncontrollable desire to give poison without regard to the consequences."

—Jane Toppan,
on her career choices in the *New York Times*,
October 23, 1904

"That is my ambition, to have killed more people—more helpless people—than any man or woman who has ever lived."

—Jane Toppan

Women are not predator animals the way men are. There are few female serial killers, and even those few that do exist are motivated often by financial reasons, but Jane Toppan was different. For her, killing was a sexual thrill, and her hunting grounds were the hospitals of Boston and the wealthy districts of Cape Cod. Such a rare murderer, especially since Toppan was the inspiration for the classic novel and movie *The Bad Seed*, deserves a closer look.

Toppan was born Honora "Nora" Kelly in 1854 (though some sources say she was born in 1857) to an alcoholic father and a mother who died when she was young. Father Pete Kelley was in no condition to raise little Nora or her three sisters. The children were taken away after Pete Kelley was found in his Lowell tailor shop, attempting to sew his own eyes shut. Nora was sent to an orphanage and eventually taken in by a woman named Ann Toppan. This was not a modern adoption, but rather "indentured adoption"—the Toppans had picked up Nora as a servant, and were they unsatisfied with her domestic service, could return her to the orphanage at any time prior to Jane reaching the age of her majority. Now known as Jane Toppan, the young girl had a better life than could have been provided by her mentally ill father, but her problems remained profound. Young Jane was jealous of her foster sister, Elizabeth, who was both beautiful and the princess of the home in which she lived. Jane began putting on weight as well, and was unpopular with boys because of her status as an indentured servant. Her "mother" Ann, abused her terribly. Despite all this, Jane appeared to be a happy child, though she was known as a fibber who made up crazy tales about her relatives—father had sailed to China, a sister was married to an English lord (in fact, she was in an insane asylum). Jane had friends, but no boyfriends.

Jane was briefly engaged in the 1870s, but her beau left her for another woman, leading to a severe depressive crisis. Jane kept to her room and twice attempted suicide, but even that was no way out. With few prospects for a suitable marriage, and thus no real means to escape the Toppan family, Jane took the one path she had—she entered nursing. With no form of sexual release available to her in those repressive times, she also took up killing.

Toppan began her training at Cambridge Hospital in 1885. Jane Toppan was a manipulator—as a nursing student under the strict regime of the time, she managed to get fellow students expelled after framing them for infractions of discipline. She also made up fanciful lies, such as her claim that she was off to work for the tsar of Russia. Soon Jane was disliked by many of her fellow nurses, but beloved by her patients and by the senior staff. With access to morphine and atrophine (a drug extracted from deadly nightshade and mandrake that would counteract morphine), she would overdose her patients and fake up their medical charts to hide evidence of their intake. For patients she liked, this was just a way to keep them with her longer—for those she disliked, she would use her skills to murder them. Thanks to her gregarious demeanor and free-spending habits, she was known by her friends and colleagues as "Jolly" Jane. Too bad Jane got her jollies from climbing into bed after she poisoned them. She would wrap her limbs around the frail bodies of her helpless charges and get sexual satisfaction—as she called it, a "voluptuous delight"—from feeling the life leaving the bodies of the patients she had poisoned. By manipulating the doses of morphine and atrophine, she was able to make her victims hang on to life for an extended period of time and one drug often disguised the effects of the other.

Despite the trail of bodies, or perhaps because the Cambridge staff simply wanted the increasingly odd Jane out of their hair, Toppan soon got a job at Massachusetts General Hospital in Boston proper. In 1890, she dared leave the ward without permission and was fired without ever receiving her diploma. Jane attempted to gain a nursing job with forged documents, but when that failed, she went into business as a private nurse for the wealthy. Her ability to navigate the world of the upper classes, learned back in Lowell in the Toppan house, served Jane well—soon she was earning twenty-five dollars a week, five times the average for women employees. And yes, sometimes her charges would die, especially if they were elderly, and indeed sometimes a few items or articles or clothing or loose cash might go missing, but certainly it wasn't the fault of Jolly Jane.

All of the asylums are rumored or confirmed to have some sort of catacombs.

In 1899, Elizabeth Toppan called on Jane. Now married, Elizabeth was experiencing a "winter melancholy" and needed a nurse. Jane invited her foster sister out to the Cape Cod cottage she was renting to relax. Never having forgotten a thousand wrongs both real and imagined—while mother Ann was cruel, according to all reports Elizabeth had always been kind to her foster sister—Jane poisoned the woman and even conned her widower out of a watch that had belonged to poor Elizabeth. But then the rent came due on the cottage, which Jane had rented for five summers, and there was only one thing left for Jane to do. Over the course of several months, she systematically murdered the members of her landlord's family, the Davises, wiping out the line entirely. First the elderly Mary Davis went to Cambridge to collect the money from Jane, in a friendly manner, of course. She returned to Cape Cod in a coffin. Daughter Genevieve made the fatal error of inviting Jane back to the Cape for Mary's funeral. Poor Genevieve was prostrate with grief, so when she died in her bed it was assumed that melancholy had swallowed her, or that she had even committed suicide. The elderly family patriarch, Alden Davis was next, but Jane's error was finally targeting healthy and young Maryanne Gibbs. Suspicions grew, but then back in Cambridge, Jane Toppan had come under suspicion for the mysterious death of one of her patients. The Cape Cod bodies were exhumed, and Jane was soon on trial for the murder of Maryanne Gibbs.

The trial was a local sensation. Jane Toppan had little to lose, ultimately, for she was still a member of the fairer sex. The mere fact that she was a killer, one who proudly proclaimed that, "my ambition is to have killed more people—helpless people—than any other man or woman who ever lived..." made it clear that she was insane. Women weren't killers; she could not have known what she had done, so went popular belief and legal theory both in 1902. She confessed to eleven murders and *The New York Journal* later ran a "confession" that claimed as many as thirty-one murders for Jolly Jane. Sentenced to the Taunton Insane Hospital, Jane lived until 1938, but not until she tried to starve herself. You see, she was worried that the nurses in the hospital might be trying to poison her.

Danvers State Hospital

It is true that I have sent six bullets through the head of my best friend, and yet I hope to show by this statement that I am not his murderer. At first I shall be called a madman—madder than the man I shot in his cell at the Arkham Sanitarium.

—H. P. Lovecraft,
"The Thing on the Doorstep"

Like the poor, the mad will always be with us. In the mid-1800s, the new urbanism and the lack of a social safety net, plus some peculiar ideas as to what caused mental illness, led to the demand to build mental hospitals to contain and treat the afflicted. In Danvers, Massachusetts, a huge and beautiful asylum, the State Lunatic Hospital was built.

While there is not as much evidence, there are many stories.

The door of a Nightmare New England haunt.

This type of evil workshop is what is rumored to lurk in older asylums.

Featuring a 130-foot tower atop the main Kirkbride building, the campus that later became known as Danvers State Hospital housed thousands of the mentally ill and unfortunate, inspired generations of authors and ghost hunters, and earned a reputation as the most haunted place in Massachusetts and the most haunted hospital in America. Even that fearsome reputation could not save the beautiful if decaying castle however, and finally the hospital itself met an ignominious end—as condominiums.

The State Lunatic Hospital was built in 1878, near the site of alleged Salem witch activity. Designed to house 600 patients of both genders in segregated quarters, the hospital looked more like a beautiful manor house with its great towers and fine detailing than a prison for lost souls. The 70,000-foot campus cost over one million dollars to build, and included its own pathology lab, a school, and even a cemetery for patients who died while in care. The progressive physicians running the place considered physical constraints—which at the time included everything from leather straps to head cages—inhumane and allowed the inmates free rein along throughout the four wings of the main building and much of the 500-acre campus.

Over the decades the asylum grew overcrowded. Designed for hundreds, it ultimately held thousands—night shifts of nine employees had to oversee 2,400 patients during the peak years of the 1940s—and though physical restraints remained forbidden, lobotomies and electroshock treatment were used to tame madmen's dreams. What was once an awe-inspiring edifice became a handy way to evoke dread. H. P. Lovecraft took Danvers as the model for Arkham Sanitarium for "The Thing on the Doorstep," his classic story of mind-transference—itself a metaphor for mental illness. Danvers is deep within "Lovecraft Country" and the author referred to Danvers proper in several other of his stories including "Pickman's Model" and "The Shadow over Innsmouth." Lovecraftians held the first of their NecronomiCons literary conventions at a hotel in sight of the haunted towers as a tribute. Fans of Batman will also recall Arkham Asylum, occasional home of the Joker and directly based on Lovecraft's vision of this New England bedlam.

Overcrowding at Danvers was solved ultimately through a shift in understanding of how the mentally ill should be treated. Beginning in the 1960s, medication and outpatient treatment became more common and the client population of Danvers State Hospital began to shrink. Widespread criticism began of how patients in asylums all over the country were being treated. In the early 1970s, the Kirkbride building was abandoned and patients moved to smaller areas. The great manor became a compelling "haunted" location for thrill seekers, urban spelunkers, and paranormal research groups. By the early 1990s, the hospital was shut down entirely. However, locals still remember apparitions and creepy occurrences. Jeralyn Levasseur grew up at Danvers with her hospital administrator father and reported to the website Haunted Salem seeing apparitions and having her bed sheets torn from her while she slept by unseen forces. Most reports of voices, clanking, screams, and lights were left unpublished and passed from teenager to teenager, or old local to newcomer though; the details of the events may come simply from the thrill of traipsing through a spooky old building in defiance of the law and common sense. Over 100 individuals were arrested for trespassing the Kirkbride building over the years, and with the turn of the millennium, interest in the hospital, and security measures surrounding it, only increased.

In 2001, the film *Session 9*, which details the fictional experiences of a team of asbestos removal specialists working in an abandoned mental hospital, was both inspired by and filmed at Danvers. Filmmaker Brad Anderson even hired some urban explorers to take him on a trip through the hospital. After the release of the film, the number of would-be ghost hunters and the number of arrests shot up greatly. Danvers was falling apart, with four-story drops not uncommon, and though the still-beautiful Kirkbride building was declared a national landmark, local preservationists were rebuffed by the state government. Danvers State Hospital would soon be no more. In 2006, developers moved in and began transforming the decaying ruin into condominiums and rental apartments, but the ghosts of the past were not yet done with the site. In April 2007, a mysterious fire tore through the construction site, destroying seven of the new buildings but leaving Kirkbride unharmed. Today, at what is now called Avalon Danvers, the state doesn't pay for accommodations, but you can rent a one-bedroom apartment in the Kirkbride building for $1300 a month. There have been some noise complaints from the new tenants, though they're not hearing the screams of the lobotomized or the howling of the damned and insane—instead, a few have groused that whenever their neighbors flush a toilet, the sound penetrates their apartment walls. The horror, the horror!

Metropolitan State Hospital

Perhaps there's something about Boston that drives people mad. Not only is the area the home to the sprawling Danvers complex, where many a local ghost story was told and the movie *Session 9* filmed, but just a few miles away lies the Metropolitan State Hospital. Founded in 1930 on a campus that crosses the borders of Waltham, Belmont, and Lexington, and closed in 1992 after a long history of treatment and mistreatment of the mentally ill patients, Metropolitan is nearly as spooky as Danvers. Like Danvers, the sprawling campus was serviced by a network of underground tunnels. Like Danvers, Metropolitan also had an on-site cemetery where the indigent dead were buried under tombstones marked simply with numbers. Metropolitan even had a children's ward in the 1960s, and many of the corpses underground are of preteen patients who never had the chance to grow up. And like Danvers, Metropolitan has had many a report of ghosts on the ground across the course of decades.

Indeed, there were reports of disembodied whispers in the tunnels, shadowy men without physical bodies sliding under doors, and a sense of being watched reported by both staffers and patients. Of course, one might expect mental patients to see things, and in those sprawling old insane asylums it was often difficult to tell the difference between the inmates and the caretakers. But then there was Melvin W. Wilson. In 1978, Wilson killed another patient named Anne Marie Davee. Wilson dismembered Davee with a hatchet and hid her body parts in shallow graves. Wilson kept seven teeth as souvenirs, which were found on his person by staffers soon after. They had also found a hatchet on the grounds, and scraps of Davee's clothing. It wasn't until two years later that Davee's disappearance was seriously investigated, though.

In 1980, state senator Jack Backman launched an investigation into Davee's disappearance and nineteen other counts of negligence. A true horror show was revealed; Wilson had buried Davee in three separate shallow graves on the grounds of the hospital, and had even built a makeshift hut where he and Davee had gotten together prior to the murder. Even Danvers doesn't have such a true gruesome tale as part of its scandal-plagued history.

Interestingly, Danvers and Metropolitan have something else in common as well: the Metropolitan campus is also being developed into condominiums and apartments by Avalon Bay Communities, which is calling this complex Avalon at Lexington Hills.

A Personal Account (as told by Renee Des Anges)

I started going to some local shows and I went to a metal show in Salem and ended up meeting this band—I don't think they're together anymore—and becoming good friends with them and this guy, Mike. He was the guitarist in the band, was really into horror stuff and ghost stuff, and so was I, so we ended up becoming close and he told me about Met State.

That was when it was still open so he actually had these band photos taken there and everyone else's was normal, whatever, but his photos—whether he was by himself or with the band—had two distinct hands, but it wasn't like…I mean, it was like a hand, like a human hand, but they were blurry. And a head by his side, like all the time.

And I was like, "Oh, c'mon, you PhotoShopped them," and he said, "No, look at the negatives. We can go get them printed again. It's just going to keep coming out like that," and he really believed in all this stuff and his other friends just laughed. Mike said he had been up on the roof when they were getting pictures taken and he saw a little kid kicking a soccer ball around in the high grass of the lawn. The hospital was abandoned and so nobody was taking care of the lawn. And so the kid was kicking the ball around and Mike shouted down to him. I wasn't there during this time—Mike told me about this later, and the little kid looked up and stopped kicking the ball and then Mike came down from the roof and the ball was there and the kid wasn't.

So he told me about his first trip there and then I was completely intrigued, so we ended up going to Met State. Oh my God, that was actually really creepy. So we went over there and he parked on a side road—you had to sneak in because it was under guard by the police—kind of in the woods. So we had to go through the woods like climbing through all this stuff.

It was fine on our way there, there was nothing weird, and then we got there and we walked around this church building and there was all this oozing stuff coming out of the wall and I thought, "What is this? Ectoplasm?" and then I caught myself: "I don't know. You've got to be kidding." I'm very open to spiritual stuff, but I was like, "All right, how could this logically be happening?" so I'm like maybe there's water damage inside the old rotting buildings…but it was coming out of the weirdest places. It wasn't coming out from where the windows were. It was bleeding out from the brick and he was like, "Oh, that's really weird," so he went over and he touched it and it was literally ooze and I was like, "Okay, that's creepy," and it was all over the church.

There was more of it on certain buildings than on others and then we found this big loading dock area where the stuff was coming down at an angle. There was a chair facing one of the loading docks, the doors, at the exact angle of the white ooze and the door was open a bit and he was like, "Oh my God, there is someone sitting there. We have to get out of here," and then he was like, "I have to show you the movie *Session 9*."

I said, "Okay." I hadn't seen it, didn't know what it was, and he's like, "No. We have to leave. That chair's really creeping me out," so he grabs my hand. At first we were laughing because we didn't see anything really, but Mike said, "There's definitely spirits here," but there wasn't anything, you know…of course spirits are around you all the time and so he was like, "No, something's not right about this. It seems unsafe or unsettling." He said, "C'mon, let's go." We started running back through the woods. As we were running, the trees on both sides were rustling like someone was chasing us…but there was nobody there.

Taunton State Hospital

Over a century and a half ago, the government of Massachusetts decided to create a second state lunatic asylum because of the large number of mentally ill patients was overwhelming the only public mental hospital in the state. In adding a second asylum to compensate for the one built in Worcester in 1833, the State Lunatic Hospital was created in Taunton, first housing patients in 1854. The new asylum was designed by the same architects who created the Worcester hospital and who later worked on the well-known spooky mental institution in Danvers. When Taunton was selected for the location, citizens petitioned against it.

The residents were overruled by the overwhelming need to alleviate the overcrowding in Worcester and the facility was built in Taunton. In the northern area of the town, the State Lunatic Hospital was placed amidst acres and acres of unspoiled rural farmland. Over the decades, more buildings were added. Domes, capitals and cornices were added. A cupola rose seventy feet into the air, offering a view of the neighboring town and many nearby streams and ponds. Central ventilation and heating facilities, sewage and water services were installed, giving the building the most modern conveniences of the time. A chapel, bakery, staff apartments and laundry services were all on site.

From the outside, Taunton State Hospital looked nowhere near as menacing as it was on the inside. Within three years of it opening, the torture and killings supposedly began. The stories that eventually came to be told about the State Lunatic Hospital are far worse than any sort of haunting.

What is alleged to have occurred at what was eventually renamed the Taunton State Hospital is far more menacing and far darker than acts of the undead because they were carried out by living and breathing humans. The stories may not be true, but they are terrifying if they are. In the historical record, there was at least one reported death at the Taunton State Hospital that was caused by the staff attacking and killing a patient—but the tales that are told are uncertain, perhaps due to a cover-up, perhaps because no one wants to know, and perhaps because the stories are merely tall tales.

What is known is that the initial idea was simple: The serenity and contemplative nature of the facility, along with the sympathetic ears of the staff, would help the deranged put the broken pieces of their brains back together. The exact opposite is suspected to have occurred. Stories say that the farthest eastern corner of the institution was used for shock treatment and also for experiments that involved soaking the mentally ill in baths of blood. A one-foot square cell had bars and a chain fence that was designed to hold the insane captive still while they were shocked with ice-cold water. It is alleged that if the cold water torture did not kill the patient, an adjoining room was used to remove their limbs and to graft the limbs onto other patients in an attempt to perfect the art of limb transplants. It is even claimed that inmates were boiled alive to see how long it took for them to perish.

If Taunton State Hospital was home to such atrocities, it sounds like some of the worst torture committed in the history of the United States. What is known is that these terrifying stories exist and are retold. Beyond the stories, the truth is not fully known and there does not seem to be any way to be sure. The idea that the mentally ill were submerged in boiling water to ascertain how the process affected their internal organs is enough to perpetuate the dark reputation of the Taunton State Hospital. However one looks at the story, it seems clear that it is lurid enough to fascinate generation after generation of macabre gossiper and ghost hunter.

The mid-1800s was a completely different era in terms of treatment for the mentally ill. From depression to autism to drug addiction, the unwell were incarcerated in places like Danvers or Taunton in the name of keeping them away from the world. Stories tell of patients fleeing the abuse of Taunton and being chopped to tiny pieces, their screams still echoing across the farmland to this very day. People reported seeing lights on inside of abandoned buildings. Electric devices supposedly failed when they were brought near the buildings.

Legends also claim that apparitions can sometimes be seen fleeing the area. Along with the reports that a person could look up to the windows and see electrical sparks racing around the room, there were ones of bloody hands clawing at the glass. As with these types of stories, they say as much about the people who tell them as they do about what might be true—but Taunton has become known as a cursed place, an unholy place where children and women are alleged to have been abducted from the community and killed. Many missing persons were supposedly last seen near the institution's grounds.

Locals think of Taunton as a city, an important part of Massachusetts' history…but the strange reports in the woods demonstrate how the suburban area may not be as domesticated as Boston. Taunton is where strange and wilder creatures are rumored to haunt the woods while disembodied laughter floats through cemeteries.

Other explanations are sometimes put forth. Having housed dangerous delinquents in its time, Taunton is known for violence and desperation. Others claim that the area's dark mystique is evidence that a cult once practiced rituals in the woods. The two legends combine in a story of how the staff members were initiates in an evil cult. In that context, the deaths are described as sacrifices to dark forces.

There are also accounts of a man fleeing across the farmland in a white robe that might be either a lab coat or a patient's gown. It seems like captors and captives would both want to escape a place as demented and horrifying as Taunton. Given the Georgian architectural style of classical revival architecture, also a Dr. Thomas Story Kirkbride design—like many of the other psychiatric institutions in Massachusetts that have inspired haunted legends—it is surprising that the State Lunatic Hospital was ever intended to be such a peaceful and serene spot.

Even today—with so much of the hospital torn down after it was abandoned in 1975, a large dome on the roof of an administrative building collapsing in 1999, and then a large fire tearing through the wings in

March of 2006—there continue to be stories that dying homeless people make their way to the Taunton grounds to exhale their last breaths. Whether it is ghosts of murdered patients or the victims of deranged sacrifices, Taunton's stories are more of human desperation and human degradation. They live on as a testament to the hideous state of mental health services in the 1850s and to the way that human depravity will always lurk at the roots of most paranormal experiences.

Someone claiming to be a former worker at the Taunton State Hospital eventually came forward and reported that tunnels with train tracks linked the buildings so that food could be shipped from the kitchen to the different buildings. He believed that the tunnels somehow hid the asylum's darkest secrets. In 2009, the demolition of the Taunton State Hospital was budgeted for 1.3 million dollars. While the official explanation is one of buildings was damaged by fire, there might be other reasons.

One cannot help but wonder if the tunnels are still there and if the trains are still running. Cult activity, a place for homeless people to die and an asylum where people were killed for fun, Taunton is clearly a place that should only be explored by professionals. If it were not designed with such noteworthy architecture, it might not even be worth remembering. Without the rumors, it would be just another haunted insane asylum. Because of the rumors, it is something far, far worse. One of the most persistent stories, through all the incarnations, is a voice telling visitors to leave. Leaving, fleeing any way possible as quickly as you can, seems like good advice…

Director of Nightmare New England and Spookyworld, Mike Krausert, is working on the Ravensclaw haunt.

My what big eyes and scabby foreheads you have.

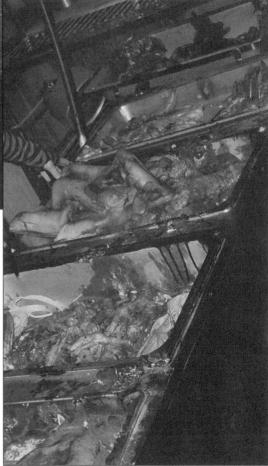

This set by Nightmare New England is enough to make anyone lose their lunch.

Chapter Seven
Stone's Public House

The rafters shake every so often at this nineteenth-century pub in Ashland, Massachusetts, thanks to the trains that roll by all evening. The Public House, which has over the years been an inn with rooms for overnight guests, a bar, virtually abandoned, and is now a modern gastropub, was built right by the railroad tracks in 1834. John Stone, a wealthy landowner had to let the rail line through his property in what was then called Unionville, but decided to make the best of it by building a place for food, drink, and sleep right by the stop. Stone only managed the inn for a couple of years before leasing it to his brother and then a succession of innkeepers and pub masters, but this haunted hideaway's supernatural reputation started with a story of the blood on Stone's hands.

Stone wasn't just a member of the landed gentry, he had been in the militia. There's an existing photograph of the man—his thick jaw, the deep folds on his cheeks and broad nose mark him as a rough customer. And, of course, pub owners in those wild days had to be ready for all manners of drunks and ne'er-do-wells. Stone may have been a wild one himself—supposedly during a high-stakes card game with his brothers and traveling salesman Michael McPherson from New York, Stone grew angry at what he believed was the salesman's cheating. Words were exchanged, and arms drawn. Stone pistol-whipped McPherson, killing him, and supposedly buried the body in the basement of the inn. Subsequent owners have even gone digging down below, but haven't found a skeleton yet. Some also claim that Stone and the maid and cook on duty at the time also haunt the place, if only to make sure that nobody finds McPherson's old bones.

There were some secrets in the basement of Stone's Public House, though—a hidden room was found behind a cement wall and in that room was found a rough cot and some ragged blankets. Stone's Public House may well have been a stop on the Underground Railroad, which repatriated escaping slaves into the free North.

Any building as old and storied as Stone's Public House will have its share of secrets, and its share of deaths. In addition to the possible murder of the salesman by the owner's own hand, the niece of one of the employees died in one of the inn's rooms after an illness. This story may also be connected to the "bloody dress" story—a waitress found a bloodied dress in the fourth floor of the building and when removed, both the waitress and her beau experienced a number of poltergeist-like experiences and effects. When the dress was returned to the trunk in which it was found, the bizarre happenings ceased. Did this bloody dress belong to the "sick" young woman, or to Mary J. Smith, a ten-year-old girl said to have been hit by a passing train car back in 1862? The Public House would be the closest place to bring someone in pain and need if there was a rail accident, after all. The upstairs function room is supposedly home to several ghosts, at least as claimed by a number of psychics and ghost hunters working independently of one another. One of the ghosts, supposedly named Burt Philips, is said to have been a frequent customer who died in the inn in the 1890s who continues to haunt the place as he enjoys.

Stone's supernatural reputation began with the purchase and rehabilitation of the inn by Leonard "Cappy" Fournier in 1976. At the time, Ashland was experiencing a bit of an economic boom, transforming itself from sleepy exurb to bustling suburb and bedroom community for the Boston metro area. The Public House certainly seemed old and almost out of place—a throwback to a time before the rise of chain restaurants and pubs with prefab ambience, to a time when an inn could be the center of the community. It's no surprise that the new owner was greatly interested in the past, in some Golden Age that could best be remembered by ghosts.

Mixed drinks with giant rocks?

And if being haunted attracted a bit more trade from curiosity-seekers and the occasional newspaper column or interview, so much the better. While Fournier may be a true believer, or he may simply be interested in the tourist dollars that ghost stories can bring, it is worth pointing out that many of the wait staff and even guests have also experienced minor supernatural events: snatches of voices from the old inn rooms (which are no longer available for letting), phantom taps on the shoulder, faucets that turn on by themselves. If there are ghosts at Stone's Public House, they are as charming and as warm as the ambience, stories of bloody dresses and long-dead cardsharps aside.

Today the Public House does not depend solely on its supernatural reputation. Live music and trivia contests are offered, and the cuisine is trendy gastropub—forget greasy wings and chips, try the soft-shell crab with mango black bean salsa and chipotle aioli as a starter, and then move on to the mushroom ragout with white polenta for the main course. Local beers such as Wachusett Ryde (an ale with a touch of rye) are available on tap. If you don't like ghosts, you can always try Stone's Public House for the spirits!

Stone's Public House
179 Main Street
Ashland, MA 01721-3124
(508) 881-1778

Haunted Massachusetts is a desolate place, but it also possesses a strange sense of beauty. *Photo courtesy of Haley A. Wright of Queen City Paranormal of New Hampshire.*

Chapter Eight

Salem and Dogtown

Salem

The Salem Witch trials are one of the most sensational legal and social events in American history, and took place before there was even an American nation. Between February 1692 and May 1693, over 150 men and women in the city of Salem and surrounding towns were accused of witchcraft, with fatal results. The colony of Massachusetts was dominated by the Puritans, a religious sect that saw no distinction between religion and the state—the Puritans also believed that Satan himself was active in the New World and constantly struggling to undermine the work of God. Today we tell school children that the Puritans journeyed to America for religious freedom, but this isn't quite the case. The Puritans wanted freedom from the Church of England, but had no interest in pluralism or democracy. They were going to rid the New World of Satan and conquer it for the Lord. The Puritans created a theocratic state as powerful and as repressive as anything seen in human history. And where there is repression, madness often follows.

Malleus Maleficarum, or The Witches' Hammer, was published by papal decree in 1486. This guide to the hunting and prosecution of witches inspired countries across Europe to make witchcraft a capital crime. However, witch hunts remained relatively rare. Of course, that there was no witch cult, despite the claims of early modern Church (and the contemporary neo-pagan movement) helped in that matter. Economic turmoil, sectarian conflict, and a widespread belief in a witch conspiracy was necessary to spark a witch hunt. The United Kingdom was, of all

Western Europe, the least swept up in worries over witchcraft, with fewer than 500 "witches" executed, and with no real search for a conspiracy of evil. However, the Puritans were the radical fringe of English culture, and now they were alone in a new continent, half-starved and surrounded by native peoples of strange habits and unheard of beliefs.

It is in this context that two young girls sparked the hysteria that to this day stains the psyche of the nation. Eleven year-old Abigail Williams and nine year-old Betty Parris began to have seizure-like fits and complained of being tortured by ghostly pains. They chanted nonsense, shrieked, and panicked, hid and cowered from invisible spirits. Deodat Lawson, a village pastor, described one of these fits in great detail:

> Abigail Williams, (about 12 years of age,) had a grievous fit. She was at first hurried with violence to and fro in the room, (though Mrs. Ingersoll endeavored to hold her,) sometimes making as if she would fly, stretching up her arms as high as she could, and crying "whish, whish, whish!" several times. Presently after she said there was Goodwife N. and said, "Do you not see her? Why there she stands!" And the said Goodwife N. offered her the Book, but she was resolved she would not take it, saying often, "I won't, I won't, I won't, take it, I do not know what book it is. I am sure it is none of God's Book, it is the Devil's Book, for ought I know." After that, she ran to the fire, and began to throw fire brands, about the house; and run against the back, as if she would run up chimney, and, as they said, she had attempted to go into the fire in other fit...

These girls were not ordinary young people either; Betty was the daughter of Samuel Parris, the religious leader of Salem, itself a city second only to Boston in the fledgling colonial system. Parris was by many accounts an acquisitive and harsh leader, a former merchant who saw no reason why his flock shouldn't acquiesce to his ever greater demands for wealth, and who exercised his power freely. By the end of 1691, some sought to withhold their tithes from the church. The year turned, and the fits began in the Parris home.

When no immediate physical cause could be found for the strange behavior of the pair, which also started manifesting in other local girls, witchcraft was blamed. Three women—the impoverished beggar Sarah Good, the outsider crone Sarah Osborne who did not attend church regularly, and the black, non-Christian slave Tituba—were accused of consorting with the devil and using their evil powers to attack the girls. Nobody cared about the rights of these women, all of whom had violated Puritan ideals in some way and all of whom matched the "profile" of a witch, so they were quickly jailed.

Perhaps it was Tituba, who made the mistake of telling the Parris girl stories of Barbados, and folk tales that involved fortune-telling, that first sparked the groundwork for the chaos to come. Indeed, according to some sources, she initially used "white magic" to try to help the hysterical girls. She made what she called a "witch cake" made from the urine of the girls, mixed with rye meal, and fed it to a dog in order to find a witch. This simple action brought Tituba to the attention of the court. Now there were even witnesses to her witchcraft. Her confession of witchcraft saved her life, but was as embroidered and as fiery as any young girl's daydream. "I ride upon a stick or pole and Good and Osborne behind me we ride taking hold of one another," she said, and she also offered up dark visions of the Devil, who frequently visited her. Did Tituba's frantic confession feed the hysteria that swept the colony, or was Parris himself the mastermind of a cultural revolution, one he believed would eliminate his political opponents permanently?

Sarah Good attempted to save herself by naming names, but it didn't work. Even her own daughter, the six-year-old Dorcas, turned against Good and claimed to have seen three evil birds Good would command to torment the afflicted. Her husband William claimed to have found a "witch's teat" (perhaps an actually existing vestigial nipple) by her right shoulder.

Sarah Osborne was also presumed to be guilty, though of course she denied it and even denied knowing Sarah Good, her supposed co-conspirator. When told that a ghostly form that looked like her had attacked the children, Osborne remarked that she did not know "that the Devil goes about in my likeness to do any hurt." For a moment, the local authorities were concerned—could the Devil take a spectral form of a local woman without that woman's acquiescence? Was she a witch, or simply bewitched? In the end, the trial went forward. Sarah Osborne had to be a witch.

The next round of accusations were even more frightening, as the afflicted girls in Salem, nearby Ipswich, and other towns fingered well-respected churchgoer Rebecca Nurse. Another church member, Martha Corey, declared that she did not believe that witchcraft was running rampant in the colony, leading to her being targeted as witch as well. She even went to the Putnam home to assure Ann that she had nothing to do with the girl's affliction, which simply gave Ann Putnam the opportunity to throw herself to the floor—" [her] feet and hands twisted in a most grievous manner and told Martha Corey to her face that she did it." A man named John Proctor also learned that to object meant to be arrested. A servant of his, twenty-year-old Mary Ann Warren tried to recant her own accusations, she tried to explain that Williams and Parris were faking their fits, but threatened with hanging she toed the line once again and allowed the hysteria to continue.

Soon, dozens of people were being arrested and examined, and many of them even confessed to practicing witchcraft, though they did so in the hope of mercy. There was never any true evidence of a witch-cult in Salem. Ultimately, nineteen "witches" were hanged in Salem and the environs, and one died while resisting the court. Many more were accused; and prisons as far as Boston began to fill with people from every social stratum. Only appeals to the Superior Court of Judicature, recently formed when a new colonial charter was granted, began to turn the tide. The influential clergyman Increase Mather took to his pulpit to decry the use of some of the more dubious forms of evidence—such as "spectral evidence"—that had taken or ruined so many lives, and slowly, perhaps out of exhaustion, or skepticism, or simply due to worry that if the trials continued they might be next, the people of Salem and the nearby towns began to listen to reason.

Spectral evidence was the key in many of the cases during the witch trials. It was believed that the Devil could only take the form of a specific human being with the permission of that human. If an accuser thus claimed to have encountered a witch, even an alibi with witnesses could be countered. Magical techniques such as a "witch cake"—Tituba had no monopoly on this technology—which, when fed to a dog, would supposedly cause pain and convulsions in a witch, was also used as evidence, as was the "touch test"—a blindfolded defendant would be made to touch an accuser. The accuser just needed to act afflicted or fake a fit, and the defendant would be considered a proven witch. Once such evidence was entered in court, there was little for the accused to do but confess and hope for a quick death by hanging rather than a slow one by torture.

One man, the wealthy eighty-year-old Giles Corey, refused to enter a plea. Without a plea, there could be no trial under the legal regime of the time. There was a solution to such obstinance, though—*peine forte et dure* or pressing. Pressing was an attempt to persuade via Corey being...

> ... remanded to the prison from whence he came and put into a low dark chamber, and there be laid on his back on the bare floor, naked, unless when decency forbids; that there be placed upon his body as great a weight as he could bear, and more, that he hath no sustenance, save only on the first day, three morsels of the worst bread, and the second day three droughts of standing water, that should be alternately his daily diet till he died, or, till he answered.
>
> (Old English Law)

Corey was crushed to death by huge rocks over the course of a day and night in order to make him plead, but he died without breaking, without saying anything more than "more weight," and finally cursing the colony itself, thus saving his large estate for his family. Mary Ann Warren had spelled his end when she claimed that his spirit visited her in the night.

The Salem Witch trials were an example of mass hysteria: irrational beliefs, economic problems, and the subordinate role of women in Puritan society all played a role in allowing nineteen people to be hanged for being witches in Salem and beyond, and nearly 150 more to be arrested (five of whom died in prison). Even two dogs were killed, after being accused of having the "evil eye." Today, a "witch hunt" is the term used for unfair and belligerent attempts to seek out wrongdoers without regard to evidence or the right of someone to be skeptical of the prosecution. The search for Communists during the 1940s and 1950s is commonly referred to as a witch hunt, as in that era the accusation of Communist Party membership was sufficient to ruin lives and careers.

Ironically, today Salem is known as Witch City. Starting in the 1970s, modern-day pagans and psychics began moving to the city, to reclaim it from the terrors of the past. The city taxis are stamped with an image of a witch, and a statue of Samantha—the witch character from the TV show Bewitched—is in the town square. Like many of the towns of the North Shore, the working class of Salem was hit hard by the end of industrial activity and the aging of the port. There remain buildings from the seventeenth century and a wonderful town square, but there are also modern homes in disrepair. The long decline of shipping has left Salem a small North Shore town of fewer than 50,000 people. But has now turned to its dark and hateful past for the sake of tourism.

There is the Salem Witch Museum on Washington Square North, which uses stage sets and dioramas to portray the witch trials. More frightening is the Witch Dungeon Museum, which features live actors and a script based on actual court transcripts of the Sarah Good trial, as well as a recreation of the dungeon where so many were tortured. The Salem Wax Museum also features horrifying images from the witch trials, and also other historical figures from that famous town. The local community theater is transformed into the Witches Cottage which shows shows about witches and the local ghosts of Salem Inn and the Ropes mansion. And, of course, for a small town of 40,000 residents, there are a more-than-proportional number of New Age shops, witch supply stores, fortune tellers, haunted tours, crumbling cemeteries, and creepy weirdos looking for a bit of magic.

Salem's tourist year culminates at the height of autumn—Halloween sees hundreds of thousands of people swarming into the small Massachusetts town to take part in parades and celebrations. On October 31st, 2001, more than three hundred years after the hysteria and brutality of the trials, Massachusetts state Governor Jane Swift signed a proclamation declaring all the Salem "witches" to be innocent. Today, Salem is a haven for the weird and unusual, a locus for the gathering of witches. After a fashion, religious freedom and tolerance has finally been achieved thanks to the bloodshed by witch hunters and hysterics.

> ### Salem Witch Museum
> 19 North Washington Square
> Salem, MA 01970
> (978) 744-1692

The House of Seven Gables

Halfway down a by-street of one of our New England towns stands a rusty wooden house, with seven acutely peaked gables, facing towards various points of the compass, and a huge, clustered chimney in the midst. The street is Pyncheon Street; the house is the old Pyncheon House; and an elm-tree, of wide circumference, rooted before the door, is familiar to every town-born child by the title of the Pyncheon Elm.

—Nathaniel Hawthorne
The House of the Seven Gables

Poe represents the newer, more disillusioned, and more technically finished of the weird schools that rose out of this propitious milieu. Another school—the tradition of moral values, gentle restraint, and mild, leisurely fantasy tinged more or less with the whimsical—was represented by another famous, misunderstood, and lonely figure in American letters—the shy and sensitive Nathaniel Hawthorne, scion of antique Salem and great-grandson of one of the bloodiest of the old witchcraft judges. In Hawthorne we have none of the violence, the daring, the high coloring, the intense dramatic sense, the cosmic malignity, and the undivided and impersonal artistry of Poe. Here, instead, is a gentle soul cramped by the Puritanism of early New England; shadowed and wistful, and grieved at an unmoral universe which everywhere transcends the conventional patterns thought by our forefathers to represent divine and immutable law. Evil, a very real force to Hawthorne, appears on every hand as a lurking and conquering adversary; and the visible world becomes in his fancy a theatre of infinite tragedy and woe, with unseen half-existent influences hovering over it and through it, battling for supremacy and molding the destinies of the hapless mortals who form its vain and self-deluded population.

—H.P. Lovecraft
Supernatural Horror in Literature

The House of the Seven Gables is haunted in life and haunted in literature. Noted American author Nathaniel Hawthorne wrote about the House of the Seven Gables in his novel of the same name and the building still stands in Salem, Massachusetts. Also called the Turner-Ingersoll Mansion, the house was constructed in 1668 and is the oldest mansion made of wood still standing in all of New England.

Hawthorne's great-great grandfather was reportedly a judge at the Salem Witch Trials and that legacy led to Hawthorne spelling his name differently in order to distance himself from his family's sinister reputation. In 1851, he wrote the celebrated book that helped cement the reputation of the famous and haunted mansion. In ruminating on guilt and atonement, retribution and the exposure of dark secrets, Hawthorne was examining the legacy of his great-great-grandfather.

When the House of the Seven Gables was first built in 1668, there were only three gables. Captain John Turner, a seaman, built his home and then expanded the structure with additions over the years. Three generations later, unable to afford the upkeep on the mansion, John Turner III sold the home to a man named Captain Ingersoll in 1780. Ingersoll continued the process of remodeling the house. When Ingersol died, his daughter inherited the building. She ran the shipping business that she also inherited from her father and, more significantly, befriended young Nathaniel Hawthorne. Susanna Ingersoll was one of the few who had faith in his writing during the early part of his career. Hawthorne spent many days with Susanna Ingersol and listened to her speak of the building's history and architectural peculiarities, such as its hidden staircase and other eccentric details.

Once Hawthorne was established as a literary success, he wrote the novel as a tribute to his friend. It is a gothic tale of a house that was haunted from the very day it was built due to financial schemes, including the perpetration of fraud by way of a stolen land deed hidden in the house, death, and witchcraft. The book was so popular that the House of the Seven Gables was purchased and restored as a public landmark. The home that Hawthorne was born in has even been moved to the same location. An open question, it seems, is whether the house is haunted by the ghosts from the story or if the real House of the Seven Gables developed its reputation because of Hawthorne's fertile imagination.

The House of the Seven Gables, at 54 Turner Street in Salem, is, as one would expect, rumored to be lived in by the unliving. Most believe that Susanna Ingersol, who lived there until she died at 72, still haunts the mansion that is listed in the National Register of Historic Places. Susanna Ingersol is presumed to be the elderly woman who roams the hallways and peers out the window. The young boy who plays in the attic may even be Hawthorne. Salem may have become touristy and more about "pop magic" than the hideous and infernal side of the occult that so horrified the Puritans of the town in the seventeenth century—but the House of the Seven Gables shows that the disquieting presence, the darker history of the witch trials and the haunted legends, is also buried like dark family secrets.

The House of the Seven Gables
115 Derby Street
Salem, MA 01970
(978) 744-0991

Dogtown

We could see no house, but hills strewn with boulders, as though they had rained down, on every side, we sitting under a shelving one. When the moon rose, what had appeared like immense boulders half a mile off in the horizon now looked by contrast no larger than nutshells or burlnut against the moon's disk, and she was the biggest boulder of all.

—Henry David Thoreau
1856, on his visit to the remains of Dogtown

Nothing but a settlement on Cape Ann, between Gloucester and Rockport, and a long one abandoned one at that. Yet Dogtown, Massachusetts continues to fascinate.

Dogtown was never a full-fledged town, but rather was just a number of homes along the roads that connected the two cities that now own the stretch of haunting, and perhaps still haunted, land. The earliest settlers of the areas began building their homes in 1693, and chose the inland spot to avoid detection by pirates and bandits. Alewife Brook allowed for a mill to operate in Dogtown, and traffic to and from the wharf on the cape brought both trade goods and ne'er-do-wells to the area. Farming was difficult, as the area is littered with boulders and rocks left by the retreat of Ice Age-era glaciers, but for more than a century the area thrived. Gloucester's wealthiest once lived in Dogtown, but soon the Revolution came and the men went off to fight for freedom and free trade. Development meant the end of the common road's primacy and the War of 1812 demonstrated that even an inland settlement wasn't proof against bombardment by modern cannons. By 1830, the town was gone, but the legends remain.

Dogtown died a slow death, but ironically it was the death that gave it a name. "Dogtown" comes from the fact that the last residents tended to be poor, and were often widowed women. They once had dogs as pets, companions, and protection against pirates and criminals as the men were off fighting the redcoats. Soon enough the dogs left their masters or were abandoned by them and roamed free across the rocks and high grasses of the shrinking settlement.

One of the last residents was Thomazine "Tammy" Younger, born in 1753 and living in Dogtown till her death in 1826. She was well-known as a local eccentric; children were terrorized by the idea of being seized by "Aunt Tam" as the locals called her, and taken away. Even as traffic through Dogtown waned, Tammy was well known for collecting private tolls—mackerel, pumpkins, whatever a team of traders had to spare— from those who passed by her property. Her home had a window whose shutters were controlled by a string. Whenever Aunt Tam heard the rumble of wagon wheels the window would fly open and she would appear to rudely demand payment for use of her land for those traveling to Cape Ann's mill.

In *The Heart of Cape Ann or the Story of Dogtown*, published by Charles E. Mann in the late 1800s, only a generation after the final ruination of Dogtown, the author declared that "no one ever refused Tammy." She was known for "verbal pyrotechnics" and her ability to launch into a "line of invective" on a moment's notice—even today such behavior is not seen as ladylike or feminine. Tammy earned a reputation as "queen of the witches" and was said to have threatened many a traveler with curses, though of course today we must simply wonder if history isn't but a game of whispers: Did Tammy threaten passers-by with curses, or did she simply open her window and curse at passers-by? Was she queen of the witches, or was that simply a somehow more civilized way of calling her the Queen Bitch of the appositely named Dogtown?

Mann notes that there were several other hints of evil around the life of Tammy Younger. With her Aunt Luce George, she was well-known on the cape proper. Luce was said to have the power to paralyze a team of oxen until exacting a tribute, and also that she would often go down to the wharf to collect fish from the boats coming in. What power did these women have over so many men? Mann reports that after the death of these women, money was found in the cellar over which their home once stood. The homestead was supposedly "the resort of buccaneers and lawless men. Fortune telling, card playing and other amusements whiled away their time." Mann even claimed that a friend of his once unearthed a snuff box, "the cover bearing a representation of a full rigged ship," that supposedly belonged to Aunt Tam (who partook of the stuff) but perhaps might have belonged to a frequent visitor from the wharf.

Was Tammy Younger a witch? Or did she and her aunt simple participate in an even older profession, one which may have also allowed them the opportunity to blackmail the traveling men they so often encountered? Perhaps they were part of another famed local tradition: an organized crime ring. Whether witchcraft or the rackets, nothing could save Dogtown from the forces of progress. Just four years after Tammy Younger's death—a fine coffin was provided, but the church bells were not rung for her funeral—the last resident of Dogtown, an African-American Cornelius "Black Neil" Finson was found half-dead in a cellar hole. After he was sent to the poorhouse, Dogtown was truly left to the dogs. By the time Henry David Thoreau visited the area in 1858, he found nothing but lonely rocks and a pair of loose oxen feeding in a swamp.

The homes collapsed or burned, but often the stone cellars, chimneys and doorstones remained. In the nineteenth century, there were few "ghost towns" in the United States, except of course for those Indian settlements and campgrounds abandoned in the face of white expansion. The area of Dogtown wasn't much for farming and once newer roads were developed was left to rot, but enough remained of the town in both local folklore and stone architecture to make Dogtown a bit of a tourist attraction. The towns and cities around Boston have always been obsessed with their own history, and Dogtown was a nearly unique—it was perhaps the first slum to be left to utterly collapse on itself. By the time Mann wrote his romantic chronicle of anecdotes and fancies, Dogtown was long gone, but couldn't be forgotten. Marsden Hartley, the modernist painter and poet, spent 1931 painting scenes of the boulders and grasses, and wrote a famous poem "Soliloquy in Dogtown." "It is a place up here" he wrote in part, "where, confess, converse, sphere and sphere, detect, rehearse, delete, and in the last complete their everlasting trend, world without end." Though desolate, Dogtown was a pleasant enough area in which to stroll and attracted tourists and lookie-loos for generations. Dogtown, as it is virtually undeveloped, has become an important element of the local area's water table.

Nearby Gloucester is home to generations of Babsons. The Babson family was a powerful one, and felt strong ties to the local area. John J. Babson wrote a book on Gloucester and nearby Dogtown, and even went so far as to dig through aging public records to determine which families had owned which homes whose cellars still remain. His grandson Roger founded Babson College and gave 1150 acres of land around Alewife Brook to the city. Babson was as obsessed with Dogtown and what it meant as his grandfather was, and a century after the little settlement embarked on a strange program. Babson didn't seek to rehabilitate the abandoned area, but rather sent unemployed woodcutters out to chisel messages into the boulders that had made the settlement so difficult to farm. In the midst of the Depression, this make-work, no matter how odd it was, couldn't be turned down.

There are all of twenty-three Babson boulders in the Dogtown Commons now, tributes to a belief in entrepreneurship and hard work scattered amidst Massachusetts's first dead slum. The first stone, the one closest to Babson Reservoir must have been exceptionally bitter for the carver: its slogan is GET A JOB. Others include HELP MOTHER, SPIRITUAL POWER, and simply WORK. One is perhaps a bit out of place simply because it is practical—it reads TO ROCKPORT. The oddest one of all has to be the unofficial motto of Dogtown and all ghost towns though:

NEVER TRY
NEVER WIN

Today, Dogtown Commons is a tourist spot open to hikers and picnickers. Narrative maps of walking tours of the 3600 acres of the area often use the Babson Boulders as landmarks, and one can also follow the paths to the ancient cellar-holes of long-dead residents such as Granny Day and Dorcas Foster. The uneven terrain and the final collapse of the houses have perhaps given local spirits no place to haunt, and certainly local ghost hunters nowhere to stay overnight, but blueberry picking and game hunting attracts the living three seasons of the year. Every winter, Dogtown returns to the dead.

Peg Wesson

Another witch associated with Dogtown, Peg Wesson, actually lived in Gloucester. There are several stories of Wesson, but the most famous is one of transformation and sympathetic magic. Wesson, by all accounts a slight woman of less than 100 pounds, lived in the Garrison House of the town, where spirits could be drunk and soldiers given a space to rest. There she entertained the men under the command of Captain Byles, who were on their way to Louisburg in Canada in 1745. Military men being what they are, by the end of the evening Wesson felt abused and humiliated by what she saw as their boorish behavior. The specifics appear to be unrecorded, but Sarah Comstock, writing in *Harper's Monthly* in 1919, wrote that "they bantered her without thought of malice, but her temper waxed from bad to worse until she uttered a terrific oath." Naturally, it wouldn't be much of a witch-story if the witch were kindly and the soldiers malevolent, but one can also imagine that women so often get the worst of it in these Dogtown-area tales. At any rate, Wesson swore to visit the troops on the battlefield. A rather odd oath, given that she clearly wanted to be rid of them.

Up in Louisburg, the troop was soon bedeviled by a crow who would swoop down upon unsuspecting soldiers. Of course, as the old Greek saying goes, all wars are won ultimately by crows as they have plenty of the dead to feed upon, but this crow was different. Even the finest marksmen couldn't bring the bird down. Soon, the soldiers remembered Wesson's oath and loaded a musket with a silver button from the sleeve of one of their number's coat. A marksman took aim and shot the bird, hitting it right in the leg.

Only after returning to Gloucester, did the soldiers confirm their hunch. According to Comstock, and most other sources, at the exact moment the silver bullet was fired, there "lay Peg the witch, crippled, powerless to mount her broomstick, by virtue of a serious fracture." And when the doctor examined Wesson's broken leg, he was extremely surprised to find a fragment of hot silver.

In *Stories of the Older Time*, written for the benefit of the New England Hospital by Ednah Dow Littlehale Cheney in 1890, the author recalled a number of other Wesson stories. Told supposedly in the dialect of the 1770s, with a framing story of a then-elderly aunt telling young girls a story, we're told that Wesson once decided to curse a local family, keeping their butter from churning. When Wesson appeared by the window, "you might churn and churn till your arms dropped off, but no signs of butter." The family gained their revenge, and their butter, when the mother took up a hot iron and dashed it into the churn, and out in the lilac bushes Wesson started screaming as if being burnt alive.

The aunt also tells another version of crow story in this same narrative, though with extra details. In addition to the great bird, the soldiers at Louisburg were troubled by "lots o' strange things…their canteens would be emptied, their guns be all bent up, and they had dreadful dreams, and cramps in their bones, and all sorts o' mischief was a-going on."

One of the young girls, after hearing these stories of Wesson, asked an interesting question: "Did the butter come any better after she died?" But her elderly aunt was too exhausted by her tale-telling to answer.

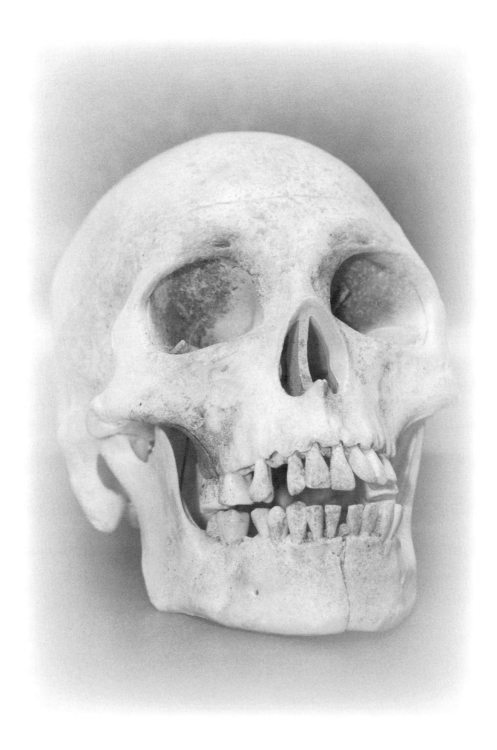

Chapter Nine
Lighthouses

All along the East Coast of the Atlantic, ghosts of lighthouse keepers can be found still tending their lights. Spirits and legends abound from Maine down through to the Long Island Sound, most likely for the simple reason that the beacon of light that saved ships in the night and fog was so important to the keepers who kept their beacons burning. Their role in protecting the ships from the cruel mistress of the sea would be hard to let go of, even from the grave. From the beginning, when fires were first lit at the edge of the sea to warn the boats away from treacherous shores or rocks, to the initial Egyptian lighthouses, ships have been guided away from danger by bright lights on the shore. Yet lighthouse keepers, as the history in Massachusetts shows, come as close to dangerous watery fates as the ships they try to guide safely to port.

Once, lighthouses used lamps with wicks as their light. The beam would travel a few miles at best, even less in inclement weather. Then, a French inventor, Augustin Fresnel, invented the lighthouse lens in 1822, which used a prism to focus the light into a tight beam. A Fresnel lens was first installed in a lighthouse in 1841. In the present day, fewer and fewer lighthouses have keepers at all—but for centuries, when a storm rolled in or fog rose up, keepers would ring bells, shoot cannons or light their giant lamps. Now, there are automatic electrical systems and humans are less involved in the process even if they are still available to check up on the operations or make repairs.

In the way that lighthouses warn sailors to straighten out their heading so that they do not run ashore or dash their boats against the rocks, many believe that ghosts are some sort of warning that should be heard or acknowledged. There is a prevailing sense that a message is being imparted. In protecting boats from beaches, islands, and harbors, the lighthouses are a beacon for ships trying to navigate in a storm or in the night, perhaps in the same way that a ghost's message is a warning. Given the similarities and the tragic and horrifying nature of shipwrecks, it is no surprise that, in having some of the oldest lighthouses, Boston also has some of the most haunted lighthouses.

Along with the five discussed below, the first lighthouse in the United States was constructed in Boston. The Brewser Island Lighthouse in the Boston Harbor first shed its light in 1716, but it was smashed to nothing but rubble in the course of the Revolutionary War.

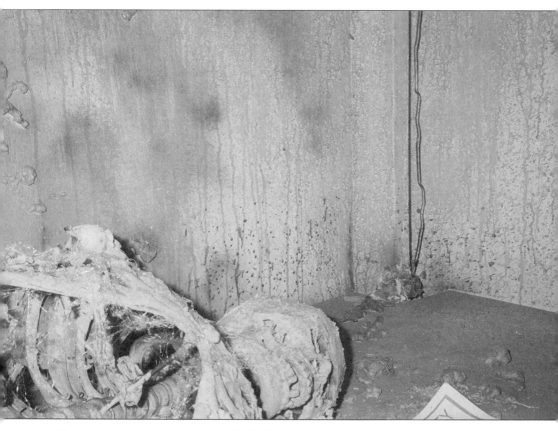

The sea takes shipwrecks, but it also takes lighthouses.

The Boston Harbor Lighthouse

The oldest lighthouse in the country that is still standing is the one in Boston Harbor. Its first tower was obliterated in the Revolutionary War. The current Boston Harbor Lighthouse was built in 1873 and then an additional fourteen feet were added to its height in 1859. Many mysterious circumstances combine in the legends of the Boston Harbor Lighthouse. There are reports that the gigantic bell that rings on days when visibility is poor cannot be heard as clearly to the east. The gap where sound is unable to carry has been called the "Ghost Walk" and has not been explained by science, despite a summer's worth of research performed by students from the Massachusetts Institute of Technology.

A ghostly presence has also been noted by more than one visitor. The story that is commonly believed is that the first proprietor, George Worthylake, is still tending the lighthouse. Worthylake perished in the water within a few months of taking the job. The second proprietor, Robert Saunders, is said to have drowned in his first week on the job. These tragic deaths have led to the rumors that Boston Harbor is haunted not just by some lighthouse keepers who live on but that the dark waters of the harbor itself are also haunted by menacing forces of the sea.

Leaving far on one side Manomet Point in Plymouth and the Scitugite shore, after being out of sight of land for an hour or two, for it was rather hazy, we neared the Cohasset Rocks again at Minot's Ledge, and saw the great tupelo-tree on the edge of Scituate, which lifts its dome, like an umbelliferous plant, high over the surrounding forest, and is conspicuous for many miles over land and water. Here was the new iron lighthouse, then unfinished, in the shape of an egg-shell painted red, and placed high on iron pillars, like the ovum of a sea-monster floating on the waves,—destined to be phosphorescent. As we passed it at half-tide we saw the spray tossed up nearly to the shell. A man was to live in that egg-shell day and night, a mile from the shore.

—Henry David Thoreau
Cape Cod

The Minot's Ledge Lighthouse

The Native American tribe known as the Quonahassitis thought that a demon named Hobomock lived among the rocks of a steep cliff about a mile out into the sea straight out from Cohasset, Massachusetts. Regardless of the type of spirit that may live in or on the rocks, there is no avoiding the simple truth that these rocks have torn open the hulls of ships for centuries.

The damage that may have been done by the demon, Hobomock, became more and more threatening over time, with increasing numbers of both ships and lives fed to the ocean, eventually leading to the construction of the Minot's Ledge Lighthouse. Noted naturist and essayist Henry David Thoreau compared the lighthouse to a sea monster coming to life because of the way it was suspended on metal legs, as if the metal tower was emerging from the ocean and clambering onto a reef.

Its keepers, even from the first day it was lit on January 1st of 1850, were afraid that the lighthouse would topple into the sea. As is always the case with such ill-starred occurrences, no one listened. The keeper was away when two assistants, Joseph Antoine and Joseph Wilson, were left to tend the light's beam. A wind from the Northeast struck so hard and directly that there was no way for the keeper to make his way back to the Minot's Ledge Lighthouse. On April 16th, 1851, everyone within miles could hear the constant ring of the lighthouse's bell. The next morning, the ocean had won once again.

One body eventually washed up on Cohasset Harbor's Gull Rock Island and the other came back to land on the island of Nantucket. No one could explain why the bell rang so incessantly as the lighthouse crumbled. Some wanted to believe that it had already fallen and waves were crashing up against the bell. Others could not help but imagine that the two Josephs were frantically signaling for help using the only method that they had available. The first construction near Scituate fell within one year. A second lighthouse with a larger and brighter light took several years to build.

In 1855, that second Minot's Ledge Lighthouse was built because the need for a beacon to protect ships had not gone away even though the first lighthouse had toppled. It was ninety-seven feet tall and went into operation in November of 1860. It proved extremely difficult to find keepers. Doors would freeze themselves shut in the winter and waves would crash up over the top of the structure. While one could imagine that the isolation led to tricks of the mind, it seems that the Minot's Ledge Lighthouse was possessed by even more sinister forces than those of the subconscious.

The first keeper lasted almost a year, but then left. Shortly after, an assistant keeper went insane, claiming that he was not able to keep from losing his mind living in rooms that did not have any corners. Shortly after that incident, another assistant keeper threatened to kill his boss. Given these experiences, it is not surprising that lighthouse employees claimed to see the phantoms of the two Josephs in the lantern room. When doors were not wedging themselves shut, there were inexplicable knocking sounds and the bell was reported to be able to ring itself in the middle of the night when no one was in the lantern room. A cat brought from town to keep them company went berserk, screeching and running around the lantern room in circles. There were even reports that, in broad daylight, the tower's reflection in the water would show two additional shadowy figures lurking near the outer walls.

In an attempt to address the problems that plagued the Minot's Ledge Lighthouse over the next one hundred and seventeen years, it was eventually automated. Yet men were seen in the now empty lighthouse, even during the worst storms. Screams were heard that were not in English and were eventually determined to be the phantom echoes of Joseph Antoine, who had originally been from Portugal.

The loneliness of the sea makes it a lovely place for a home.

The Plymouth Lighthouse

At Gurnet Point, in Plymouth, Massachusetts, the Plymouth Lighthouse was built on land owned by a couple named John and Hannah Thomas. They became the Plymouth Lighthouse's first keepers and shared the duties of the job until John was killed in the Revolutionary War. Hannah Thomas then became the first woman who kept a lighthouse by herself in the United States. Perhaps cognizant of the historical triumph of her responsibility, Hannah's spirit still lives in the lighthouse.

The Plymouth Lighthouse, like the Minot's Ledge Lighthouse, has had to be rebuilt. First erected in 1769, the thirty-four foot structure has been knocked down several times. With its tragedies, its ghostly experiences have escalated. Even in the past few decades, the top half of a woman's body was seen floating across the bedroom of the keeper's house. A photographer who spent the night there described the woman as having tragic eyes and dark hair that went down passed the legless apparition's shoulders. The guess, of course, is that this is Hannah Thomas, but the apparition has not been identified with any certainty and the photographer did not manage to capture pictures.

Bird Island Lighthouse

In Buzzard's Bay, the twenty-nine-foot-tall Bird Island Lighthouse is near Marion, Massachusetts. It has existed since 1819 and was recently renovated by a local preservation society. About a decade after it was built, a former pirate named Billy Moore was hired to keep the light. He and his wife lived there together. Mrs. Moore was known for her love of smoking tobacco. Local citizens from Marion would come and give her tobacco when they visited Bird Island. Mr. Moore never liked that his wife smoked because she coughed and never looked well. The people from Marion kept bringing her the tobacco because she looked so pale and haggard—at the time, tobacco was still seen as having health benefits by some— and even those wiser than average might have tried to at least feed Hannah Moore's addiction to the leaf to keep her going.

Eventually, she had black eyes and bruises. Finally, on a particularly chilly morning in February of 1832, the distress flag was hoisted above the Bird Island Lighthouse. When the citizens came out to the island, Hannah Moore was dead. According to her husband, the smoking had finally ended her breathing for good. The people from Marion believed him. He elaborated by saying that her condition was probably tuberculosis and he had buried Hannah almost immediately on the shore of the beach.

The bit of shore where Mrs. Moore was buried was the only ground that was not too frozen to be dug into and was thereby used for the impromptu funeral. Word got to the Marion sheriff and he decided to investigate, but Billy Moore had disappeared for good before anyone caught up with him. Unlike some lighthouse hauntings, where it takes many years for the ghost to make its presence known, Mrs. Moore returned to the structure shortly after she was buried, perhaps because it was so easy for her to claw her way up out of the sand. The replacement keepers quit because they could not tolerate how the previous keeper's wife's ghost showed up and knocked on their bedroom door in the middle of the night.

The problems from the spectral world continued, with people describing an old woman with stooped shoulders who would frighten children as she reached toward them with her ghostly arms. The keeper's house was eventually destroyed, but Mrs. Moore's ghost still haunts Bird Island and the nearby areas. In 1982, a fisherman from Marion saw her floating across the frozen harbor, still smoking her corncob pipe.

Over time, the ocean takes a piece of everything.

Baker's Island Lighthouse

Five miles off the coast of Salem Harbor there are fifteen islands that are known as "The Miseries." Baker's Island is fifty-five acres of land. There are old houses with high ceilings and long, wide porches. Wealthy elites from in and around Salem spend their summers there. Baker's Island has little more than a general store, a pump house, and the Baker's Island Lighthouse. Two lighthouses were originally built on Baker's Island in 1859. The shorter of the two was taken down in the 1920s.

Unlike the other four of the most haunted lighthouses near Boston, no one knows where the various spirits that haunt Baker's Island come from. The foghorn goes off unexpectedly on nights when fog cannot be seen for miles. The Coast Guard has been brought in but none of the equipment has needed repair. The keeper noticed that such "malfunctions" never happen during the day.

Chase Cottage

Many of the summer homes also have documented paranormal activity. The largest building on Baker's Island, the Chase Cottage, is known to have evil presences and blurry spots floating through the old building's long hallways. A family member says that she has also heard of the "Beast of Baker's Island." Research on Baker's Island has been thwarted by the lack of electricity and because the island is less inhabited in the winter. Parties, kissing noises, and music from previous eras are often reported to have been heard by winter caretakers. Putting together the various pieces, it seems that the Baker's Island lighthouse's foghorn is not going off in the middle of the night for no reason. It is communicating a loud and clear homing signal for members of various ghost societies who use the near-empty mansions to hold their midwinter parties and balls.

It can be hard to live in a place without corners.

Chapter Ten
Cape Cod

The lone spectator of this frightful scene, the only white man on the island, arose from his hiding place in the grass and fled, but he handed the story of that night's horrid work down to later generations, who have sought for the treasure in vain.

The experiences of such of the treasure seekers as have dared to tell them have been quite as terrible as were those of the Peeping Tom who saw the pirates bury their gold. Two such adventurers agreed to meet one night at the rock, the hour being that when "the ghost from the tomb affrighted shall come, cal'd out by the clap of the thunder." The first to arrive leaned up against the great stone and, being tired with his tramp, was fast falling to sleep, when a noise came to him from off the waters (for the haunted spot is close by the shore of Cape Poge Pond) and, opening wide his eyes in astonishment, he saw "a great big old ship," with all sails set, standing straight in toward the rock. No man was at the wheel, nor a soul in sight, yet she dodged the shoals and shallows like some old fisherman, and just as she must have grounded, down came every sail, and the vessel drifted gently in until her keel touched lightly on the sandy shore.

Left:
Natasha and Chase DeNamur. *Photo courtesy of Jayna Lloyd of Jayna Sullivan Photography.*

Then a mysterious plank ran out of itself and, with a horrible yell, the hatch was thrown off, and on the instant the deck was swarming with skeletons. "Twas an all-fired dark night, but it seemed as if them critters carried their light with them, for I could see 'em plain enough," says the treasure hunter. Now they come filing down the plank, bearing a dead body, and begin to dig, but the earth seemed to come up of itself, for almost instantly there was a deep hole and the spades were striking something that gave back the ring of metal, which a peep showed was a big iron pot with lid half off, and filled to the brim with gold and silver. On top of this the corpse is tumbled and the hole is being filled when, for the first time the skeletons catch sight of the intruding human, who has been scared so stiff that he could not run, and they came for him "as thick as bees," grabbing him with intent to put him in the hole to keep company with the corpse. But if his legs would not work his lungs would, and he gave such a ghastly screech that even the ghosts were frightened and dropped him so that his head fell with a bang against the rock. When he "ris to his feet" not a phantom was in sight, the ship was gone and all signs of digging obliterated. Our adventurer had had enough, however, and when his companion arrived all was dark and lonely. The deserted one, however, was not the kind to take such treatment quietly, and when next the two met he gave his terrified friend such a drubbing that in order to justify his run away he was compelled to tell his experiences, and so the facts, which would otherwise have been lost, have been preserved for posterity.

Others have tried, and even reached the pot, but always is there a horrible flash and a cave in, shadowy forms of threatening aspect and the blackness of darkness, with the hole leveled and no sign of digging to show for the night's labor. Some there be who claim that a stranger whose heel prints showed a curious cleft did secure the pot, and transported it and himself to unknown parts on a mysterious vessel that had been hovering on the horizon for days, and it may be so, for recent digging fails to cause any unusual disturbance, except possibly in the backs and muscles of the diggers.

—Charles Gilbert Hine
The Story of Martha's Vineyard (1908)

Daggett House

Cape Cod shares some interesting values with Salem. Cape Cod was also founded on Puritan principles, but also a sense of rugged individualism. The primary difference between the two settings is the spray of salt from the ocean. To those living to the west of the Cape Cod Canal, life is haunted in a slightly different way than on the Cape. Seventy miles out into the Atlantic, Cape Cod is one of the most beautiful and fascinating peninsulas in the United States…and it also has particularly distinctive myths that come along with its history.

The most interesting of the Cape Cod stories involves roving ghosts of two brothers and a dog. One of the brothers and the dog were trapped in a small room and starved to death. The other brother died from pneumonia. At 59 North Water Street, the Daggett House Inn is in Martha's Vineyard and the Daggett House Inn is known for apparitions and moving objects, commonly believed to be these two brothers and their dog. By most of the evidence, there appears to be poltergeist activity at the Daggett House. It is also considered a prime spot for future research to better understand the presence that is haunting the location. Particularly, the sounds that are otherwise hidden in static or background noise but resemble speech when recorded and amplified (called EVPs or Electronic Voice Phenomena), are often purported to be recorded here.

Simmons Homestead Inn

In Hyannisport, there is a bed and breakfast called the Simmons Homestead Inn. A sea captain, Lemuel Simmons, built the building in the 1800s. To this day, dozens of stray cats roam the grounds, most likely drawn to the area because of its confluence of otherworldly energies. Inside the building, the "Owl Room" is sometimes home to the ghost of a young girl named Susan who is somehow connected to the feline energies of the roaming cats in a way that is not yet fully understood. Susan is believed to seek out people who are particularly psychic or intuitive and make her presence known to them. Many have tried to figure out what the young girl is trying to say or communicate, but no one yet has managed to understand the message she is trying to convey.

Yarmouthport Inn

Yarmouthport is home to the eponymous Yarmouthport Inn. The Yarmouthport Inn is the oldest inn on all of Cape Cod, dating back to the 1600s. At 223 Route 6, the inn was a stop on the Underground Railroad that African-Americans followed to escape slavery before the United States Civil War. Slaves who found freedom in Massachusetts are known to revisit the spot from beyond the grave. The ghosts of the slaves are often seen wearing their tattered clothing from the 1800s. The Quisset Harbor room of the Yarmouthport Inn is best known for sightings of paranormal activity.

Barnstable House

Of all the others, the House of Eleven Ghosts deserves the title of the most haunted spot in Cape Cod. Also called the Barnstable House, 3010 Main Street in Barnstable is a place where black clouds and floating balls of light are commonly seen. The Barnstable House was built in 1716 by James Paine, a descendent of one of the famous signers of the Declaration of Independence, Thomas Paine. There is an underground river beneath the building and an owner's daughter is said to have drowned there. Later, Edmund Howes, another owner, is said to have hanged himself from a tree near the building. Dr. Samuel Savage reportedly owned the building and practiced black magic there. Little is known of the Samuel Savage name's role in the legends other than that the tombstone can be found in the area. Psychics have analyzed the various spectral energies and placed a total of eleven ghosts as spending substantial time in the building, hence its name.

The Barnstable House, the House of Eleven Ghosts, is an inn and has sometimes been a restaurant. Many times over the years, patrons have reported being approached by people in ancient clothing. A spirit named Captain Grey is said to slam doors and live in the building's dark and damp cellar. Most of all, there is a possibility that one of the most notorious ghosts of Cape Cod is linked to the Barnstable House: the Lady in Black. The Lady in Black is often seen walking the streets of Barnstable at night, disappearing once she is noticed. The Lady in Black has been hunted and stalked but she always reappears. Her legend comes in many forms, most of which are tied to Fort Warren, but the fear of her reputation lingers on. It would only make sense that one of the longest-lasting spectral forces of Boston would eventually come to Cape Cod and become connected to such a haunted building.

The Marsh People

Some other examples of Cape Cod ghost lore are less centralized. The Marsh People have long been rumored to populate the Cape's marshes. The Marsh People are believed to be humanoid yet not quite human. While it was once commonly accepted that they were descended from an isolated human bloodline that had mutated, it now seems much more likely that they are a lesser known or even previously unidentified type of undead or spirit creature.

Finally, a commonly told story about of Cape Cod is one of two sisters whose automobile broke down in the early 1900s. It was late at night and a storm had rolled in from the ocean. With no one else around, the two sisters had no choice but to approach a forbidding house in ill repair. The sisters crept up to the door and pulled the bell's cord.

When no one answered, they sneaked around the building looking for some sort of way to get inside and find shelter. The sisters peered in through a broken window while the shutters banged in the storm's cold wind. The sisters saw a room filled with dust and a library that looked like it had been untouched for quite some time.

With no other choice, stranded alone in the night, the sisters decided to gather blankets from the car and sneak inside the abandoned house. Planning on calling for help for their broken automobile on the next day, they crept in through the window, making giant footsteps in the thick layers of dust. The sisters cleared space on couches and went to sleep, cold and wishing they had the ability to start a fire in the fireplace.

Hours later, the sisters were woken by a sudden whooshing noise. A sailor, soaking wet, was standing in front of the fireplace also hoping that a fire would light and give off enough heat to dry his soaked clothing. The sailor himself gave off a greenish luminescent glow. The older sister, almost choking with fear, shouted, "Who are you? Who is there?"

The sailor made a noise, somewhere in between a moan and indecipherable muttering. The sisters moved to one couch and huddled together, eventually deciding that they had somehow shared a nightmare. Upon awakening, there was a puddle of saltwater by the fireplace. A strand of seaweed was floating in the water left on the floor.

Despite the evidence that the soaking wet sailor may have been more than a nightmare, there were no other impressions in the thick layers of dust other than their own footprints. The sisters saved the seaweed as a memento of their fearful night.

Frightened, the sisters fled the house and went back to their car. They were towed to a nearby village by a motorist who drove by. As someone repaired their car, the sisters asked around about the abandoned house where they had spent the night. The story they uncovered was that the house had been empty since well back into the previous century. A father had thrown his son out of the house and then the son had drowned. The family moved far away from Cape Cod because of strange and eerie occurrences that seemed to visit in the night.

Months later, the sisters told the story of their harrowing night in the abandoned house. At the climax, as one told of finding the pool of saltwater in the morning, the other brought the strand of seaweed from her pocket. A curator from a local museum recognized the particular type as a very rare seaweed that had only been discovered several times before. Each and every time, this particular type of seaweed was only found clinging to dead bodies...

Nantucket

Twenty-two miles off from the southernmost shore of Cape Cod, on the southeast tip of Massachusetts is where one finds the particularly haunted island of Nantucket. The town called Nantucket is on the northern shore of the island of Nantucket. Amidst the island's charm and history, there are also reminders of the more troubled elements of its past and reminders of the strange interactions between the world in which we live and the world of the paranormal. There are two houses in Nantucket that are the most well known for ghostly activity, the Jared Coffin House and the Jethro Coffin House.

Jared Coffin House

The place to start on any trip to haunted Nantucket is the Jared Coffin House. The Jared Coffin House was built in 1845 and it is one of the longest-standing large structures on the island. The building was the first mansion with three stories that was built on Nantucket Island. Now, the Jared Coffin House is a hotel well-known for its Chinese food—but the Coffin House certainly has a darker and stranger history to go along with its present-day reputation.

The story goes that Coffin, whose name obviously has something to do with the notoriety, built the dream home for his wife but that she ended up disliking how Nantucket was so far from the hoity-toity echelons of Boston high society that she so desperately wanted to be involved with. Another explanation was that Jared Coffin was accused of embezzling funds to afford his wife's expensive tastes, and though he was eventually proven innocent, it was not before the allegations ruined his reputation. Regardless, the result is that circumstance led to Jared Coffin selling or losing the house and the couple moving back to the heart of Boston. Both versions, obviously, point the finger at his wife and her yearning for more than Nantucket Island could provide.

When the Great Fire tore across the town a little over a year after the Jared Coffin House was built, the giant brick and slate building played a heroic part in finally bringing the fire to an end by stopping the fire from spreading because the bricks and slate were unable to burn.

As the Jared Coffin House has been expanded and renovated, effort has been made to retain its authentic flavor. Some speculate that the changes over the years are why Jared Coffin comes back because Coffin is checking to see how his handiwork has been altered. Along with the story of Jared Coffin returning to visit the mansion that he barely ever got to live in, it is often mentioned that the décor has been kept true to the details of Nantucket style that Jared Coffin put into building his mansion. This must be why Jared is reported to enjoy putting his feet up in rocking chairs and marveling at how well built the details of the mansion are. Jared Coffin is finally able to enjoy the home that he built now that he and his wife are both dead.

Jethro Coffin House and the Sherburne Inn

The other Coffin House is the oldest on the island, the Jethro Coffin House. It is the less frequently haunted of the two, though there is evidence that having two different haunted houses both known by the macabre name of the Coffin House have led to an intermingling of the stories over the years. Another haunted inn is the Sherburne Inn, an historic hotel in the first settled parts of the city.

Tragedies at Sea

The other haunted legend of Nantucket is the murky depths that have devoured so many boats over the years. Tragedies at sea have always been a part of Nantucket's history. The whaling ship *Essex* lives in infamy because the crew had to resort to cannibalism and the *Andrea Doria*, an Italian ocean liner, sank off the coast in 1956—showing that the watery grave off the coast of New England is at its hungriest off the shores of Nantucket. Be it the brutal, cruel, and dangerous practice of whaling or the widow's walks that are common on the roofs of many of the older salt-ridden and wind-battered houses that are known as Nantucket Grays, the waters teem with a sense of death. If one looks out long enough to the hungry sea, one sees shipwrecks floating. If one looks up to widow walks often enough, it seems likely that they will eventually see one of the tragic reminders of the women who paced the roofs with telescopes pointing out to the hungry sea with prayers on their lips.

Setstills

Finally, in Nantucket, one can find what is one of the most impressive spooks in all of New England: the setstills. Setstills are spirits known to sit on the fences of the cemeteries on the island. They sit on their fence perch and then grab and terrify people who walk by. People say that school children make sure to walk on the other side of the streets because the setsills lie in wait. The Old North Cemetery is best known for setstills and has some of the oldest tombstones on the island. By investigating that known hotspot, a curious folklorist or parapsychologist will be able to determine if Nantucket is home to a unique type of spirit that is almost unknown in the rest of the world or if adults merely made up a story to keep children from dawdling when they traveled past cemeteries.

Someday, we will all be skeletons.

Massachusetts has many cemeteries.

Chapter Eleven
Cemeteries

Boston Common

It is said that history is written by the winners, but in fact history is simply written by the living. The dead may be honored or despised or ignored, but their place in the world is almost always obscured. The centerpiece of Boston, the Common (and the nearby Central Burying Ground) is perhaps the perfect example of this truth. The Boston Common is today a lovely park that features music such as the Boston Lyric Opera's Outdoor Opera Series, the Commonwealth Shakespeare Company's Shakespeare on the Common, public rallies, the annual New Year's Eve countdown, and all array of events. The Common, however, is also a huge and nearly forgotten tomb.

Boston Common was founded in 1634 and was a true common—locals used it as a collective cow pasture until overgrazing threatened the ecology of the park. Soon the Bostonians found another use for the area—hangings. First a tree known as the Great Elm and sometimes as Boston's Oldest Resident, bore the rotten fruit of the Boston hanged, but by 1769 a proper gallows was constructed. Hangings continued in the park till 1817, and the Elm, which also held "lanterns of liberty" in its branches placed there by patriots during the Revolutionary War, was finally brought down by a gale in 1879.

Most famous of the seventeenth century hangings was Mary Dyer, a woman who violated both secular and religious law by studying the Bible with a group of her peers rather than simply accepting the law and scriptural interpretations of the Massachusetts Bay Colony. Dyer was banished from the Boston colony in 1638, and settled for a time in Rhode Island. That punishment was not enough for Governor John Winthrop, who exhumed the body of Dyer's stillborn baby and used it as evidence for heresy. He described the body as follows:

> It was of ordinary bigness; it had a face, but no head, and the ears stood upon the shoulders and were like an ape's; it had no forehead, but over the eyes four horns, hard and sharp; two of them were above one inch long, the other two shorter; the eyes standing out, and the mouth also; the nose hooked upward; all over the breast and back full of sharp pricks and scales, like a thornback [the fish now called a ray or skate], the navel and all the belly, with the distinction of the sex, were where the back should be, and the back and hips before, where the belly should have been; behind, between the shoulders, it had two mouths, and in each of them a piece of red flesh sticking out; it had arms and legs as other children; but, instead of toes, it had on each foot three claws, like a young fowl, with sharp talons.

Dyer continued following the implications of her faith and, in England, joined the Quakers. She defied her banishment and returned to Boston in 1857, a Quaker preacher in her own right. She was again arrested and banished, but continued to preach Quakerism across the Puritan colonies. A third defiant trip into Boston led to the hanging death of a number of Quakers on the great oak of the Boston Common, but Winthrop, the "monstrous birth" he had supposedly witnessed aside, granted Mary Dyer a reprieve while the rope was even around her neck. This only led to a fourth attempt to breach the colony by Mary Dyer, and she too was finally hanged on May 31, 1660. "She did hang as a flag for others to take example by," said a member of the court, and indeed the Common's most popular spectator sport was watching executions for nearly another century. Mostly treeless and still occasionally home to cows chewing their cud, the Common was also a burial ground for paupers and criminals. Though often presented today as a citadel to freedom—for a long time one didn't need a permit to hold a rally or protest in the Common—and as the place where the ideology of American individualism and democracy were so ferociously argued, the Common was the final, and painful, resting place of the poorest and most desperate of criminals, and for people like Mary Dyer who dared follow their consciences rather than the dictates of a theocratic state.

The Common is filled with the bodies of the hanged. Whether by the Great Elm or on the gallows, the bodies of the hanged were not released to next of kin...unless the family members admitted publicly that the deceased was guilty of the crime. Otherwise, the corpses were unceremoniously thrown into the Charles. Given the large number of hanging offenses, and the number that could leave the deceased barred from Christian burial grounds, often the families had no alternative but to steal the bodies of their relations in the middle of the night and quickly bury them in shallow graves elsewhere in the Common.

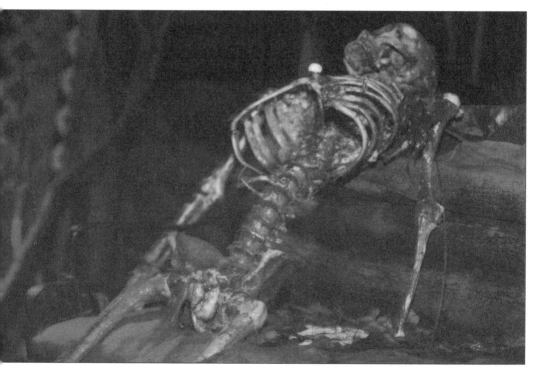

This skeleton is a prop from Nightmare New England.

The centuries have seen significant construction around the common—an underground parking lot, subbasements for elevator buildings, and of course Boston's famous "T" subway system's Green Line. Virtually every excavation project brings up skeletons and rotting corpses; some sources claim that as many as 800 bodies have been exhumed, mostly accidentally, over the years. The Green Line is especially famous for the number of bodies, many of which were mangled, missing limbs, or had shattered skulls, that turned up when the shovels hit the dirt. The subway system goes right through what was a mass grave of British soldiers slaughtered and swiftly disposed of during the Revolution. And when the trains started rolling under the common, train conductors reported seeing hazy figures in red coats running across the tracks between Boylston and Arlington Streets, and the trolleys would sometimes stall out on that very spot. Of course, the mass grave had been a news story, and the underground trolley technology was new at the time, as Boston's subway system was the first in the country. But still…

A more pleasant paranormal experience might be had in the adjacent Public Garden. Like the subway system, it's another first—a public botanical garden, still free, its twenty-four acres set aside for smelling the roses back in 1837. It's a happy place, where statues of the ducks from *Make Way for Ducklings* attract toddlers and kids, and where stands plants and trees of all varieties, including a California redwood. There's also a monument to ether—yes, the anesthetic. Even the ghosts in the garden are dreamy. There are frequent reports of two women in Victorian dress having a picnic or strolling down the shaded paths or sitting on a bench. They wave to passers-by and then vanish. Of course, skeptics point out that given the number of historical tour groups featuring guides in period dress from the colonial and Victorian eras, that these ghosts might just be pranksters or cases of mistaken identity. A welcome relief from the dark history of the Common proper, if so.

Attached to the Common is the Central Burying Ground, which though ancient is not very often celebrated. It was the graveyard for "Roman Catholics and strangers dying in the town," but also is said to contain the bodies of British soldiers slaughtered during the Battle of

Bunker Hill. Its most famous inhabitant is Gilbert Stuart, the famous portrait painter. (Indeed, Stuart is so famous that we can guarantee that you have several of his works in your possession —his is the image of George Washington on the dollar bill.) Just across the street is a plaque honoring Edgar Allan Poe, the Boston native who despised the city and denounced the Common as nothing but a frog pond.

Graveyard lovers would be better off to walk down Tremont Street to the nearby Granary Burying Ground. The city's third oldest cemetery was founded in 1660, and was originally part of the Common. The old cemetery contains a memorial obelisk dedicated to the parents of Benjamin Franklin (who is buried in Philadelphia), as well as the graves of Paul Revere, John Hancock, and Robert Treat Paine.

Victims of the Boston Massacre are also interred at the Granary as are more than 2500 nameless dead. Though the burial ground contains 2340 stones and markers, there are more than 5000 dead cramped in the small burial ground. That is the true story of Boston—it's a city that celebrates its glorious history and honored role in the founding of America, but in the end, even the most beautiful of its parks and renowned of its monuments are built upon a foundation of the anonymous, the forgotten, the dead.

The Seven Gates of Hell in Athol

Although one is pure of thoughts and in heart, searches for the gates of the truly dead. You never know when the winter winds (November) blow, If the cursed gates are searching for you too. If you enter the gates backwards you might have a small chance, to flee with your life all intact. But if your motives are untrue then the living death calls your name, then there is nothing you can do.

Instructions thought to have been given by
Madame Marie Laveau,
Louisiana Creole practitioner of Voudou
renowned in New Orleans

A lost or hard-to-solve mystery of Massachusetts is the Seven Gates of Hell. The Seven Gates is fairly prevalent in contemporary legends throughout the U.S.

Pennsylvania and Virginia also have residents who claim to know the general locations of secret entrances to Hell, but one of the better known of the "secret" locations scattered across the country is in Athol. Not unlike the dreaded and cursed volume of dark secrets, *The Necronomicon*, people claim to have found the Seven Gates of Hell in Athol—but no one living seems to be certain that the Gates (or a real version of that unholy book) really exist. The Seven Gates of Hell in Athol are supposedly off of a road called Pleasant Hill…yet research has confirmed that Pleasant Hill Road has never appeared on an Athol map.

From there, the story goes that a cult was located about 400 yards from the road. Through human and animal sacrifice, a gateway to Hell was somehow constructed. A consistent thread of all the stories is that there are seven gates that one must find and step through, sometimes in a specific pattern, in order to cross out of this world and into Hell's realm or dimension.

In Athol, the seventh gate does the trick but some of the other stories claim an eighth gate must then be found. Cutting through a clearing supposedly leads to the haunted house where the cult once lived. Blood is said to still stain the walls. There are voices, apparitions (sometimes said to be animals or people hanging from trees) and screams that can be heard all the way to the road.

The cult seems to be described in two distinctly different ways, a black magic Satanist group and a corrupted "flower power meets Charles Manson" group. The "hippies gone bad" incarnation of the legend purports that the unwary may hear a panflute playing in the woods. The sound of the flute cannot be recorded in any medium even when it is heard clearly by human ears. The Satanic sacrifice cult is more closely tied to the gates themselves because they are usually described as building the Seven Gates to Hell. The hippy commune is described as accidentally uncovering the evil gates and then being taken over by the malevolent and hypnotic power they unearthed.

None of the stories are quite sure of the secret attributes of each gate, but the belief is that each gate either takes something from the person who crosses through it or unleashes some sort of demonic entity. Passing through the first gate leads to something like seeing darker shadows or hearing dogs and wolves howl until ghosts and demons start to appear… eventually the person crosses into Lucifer's realm or the demons come through to "our" world.

Some people say that only the first three gates have been found so far, others say five, and some even go on to say that all seven are in the general Athol area but that the evil consequences will only come to pass when a single individual randomly walks through them in the right order. Bedford, Virginia's version of the Seven Gates of Hell legend says that slaves were killed and all the gates are made of black iron. New Orleans, Louisiana's account and the one from Stull, Kansas, take on the particular nature of their locations too. New Orleans gets linked to voudou and Kansas's Stull Gates of Hell are located near Lawrence, Kansas (home of the Kansas Jayhawks college team) and were often sought by people celebrating Jayhawks victories at keg parties out in the woods. At Stull, broken glass bottles were found so frequently that visiting the rural cemetery was strongly discouraged. Sometimes the location is said to be near Route 666.

Given how this story is of a more recent vintage than most regional ghost stories, it is an ideal example of how the folklore of today fills a certain space that was once held by mythology of the past. Fairy tales seem rooted in an earlier time, or symbolic, but the Seven Gates of Hell has people looking for them on a map, even if only so that they can go there and prove that they are not scared.

That people want to know the truth and want to consider opening the door is also a part of the modern, post-superstitious world. People love the idea of locking evil away and people love the idea of setting evil free. "Abandon hope all ye who enter here!" can be a warning but it can also be comforting because the ruse of hope can be so tiring to maintain. In considering how the idea of Gates to Hell being found in Massachusetts ties into older folklore, it seems more like how the legend of *The Necronomicon* functions…it is secret and hidden knowledge that tests the knower's mettle.

Given the dangers that would be lurking on the other side for anyone who could actually open a gate to Hell, it would be important to know of Charon, Hermes, and the river Acheron. It would be important for any explorer to have a few coins to pay their way. It would be worth taking the time to learn the names of Lucifer or how to obtain a golden bough—but that is unlikely to be occurring. Kids who are seeking the Seven Gates of Hell in Athol are legend-tripping and they are finding their own meanings in the powerful myths. They do not know Erebus and Nyx and they might not recognize Cerberus even if they were bitten by each of his three heads—but they know that people die. They know that there is darkness. They know that they want to see what Hell is really like.

Spider Gates

Boston's cemeteries are not actually the most haunted in the state. The ones that are farther out toward the center of Massachusetts are the ones that attract the legends. Spider Gates Cemetery in Leicester is another prominent example of an out-of-the-way legend. Like the Seven Gates in Athol, it is a location where an "Eighth Gate" is rumored to exist. Unlike the Seven Gates, Spider Gates is a real cemetery and a real place, so the location can legitimately be found out past brush and farmland.

In considering how these stories form, it is interesting to speculate why they take hold in certain places and why they do not in others. Spider Gates has an interesting name and distinct wrought iron gates. Looking at Spider Gates from the outside, this particular place is the kind of setting that looks like evil might take hold. On the inside, conversely, Spider Gates is a place of serenity and manicured grass.

It is privately owned and dates back to the 1700s. The real name is The Quaker Cemetery though it is also sometimes called The Friends

Cemetery. The graves are taken care of and kept neat. Ghost hunters are discouraged from going to the location by modern-day Quakers, but those that did would find little more than a pleasant picnic. A handmade stone wall goes around the outer perimeter. There are simple traditional tombstones. A debate persists between whether Spider Gates just has a bad reputation because of its name and front gates or if it too may have been home to another (or perhaps even the same) band of Satanists who are said to have worked black magic in Athol. Some claim a flat rock slab in the cemetery was used for ritual murders and others say that it was the foundation of an abandoned Quaker meeting place.

The ghosts that are most often placed at Spider Gates are those of children who were supposedly beaten to death and then had their bodies hidden in a small culvert on the cemetery grounds. In terms of gates, Spider Gates has only one real entrance and three gates at most. The metal gates look like a spider's web or light radiating out from a sun, but there is little else that is out of the ordinary. Despite looking serene and seeming like an unlikely cemetery for such dangerous hauntings, there are also reports of black-robed worshippers who chant and sacrifice goats. It is a strange combination, a secluded Quaker cemetery and some sort of sacrificial charnel house.

Given the juxtaposition, the strange reputation of Spider Gates cannot just be because of the unique artwork of the gates. Another of the stories is that a teenage boy hung himself from a tree by the front entrance. Others claim that certain areas are unable to grow grass or even that strange creatures howl in the nearby woods. There have even been reports of a second hidden cemetery or a white substance that oozes up from the ground, but those reports are infrequent.

The cemetery, on Earle Street, is hard to find, best located by driving up Manville Street from the entrance to a landfill. Kettle Brook is nearby. The gate faces due north and it does seem that the walls are aligned based on the cardinal directions. With only one set of gates, it makes sense that these would be the "Eighth Gate." Newspapers and other sources do not seem to back up any of the accounts of violence. Despite the online attention that this particular graveyard attracts, it seems to be a private

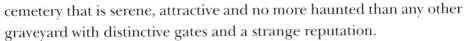

cemetery that is serene, attractive and no more haunted than any other graveyard with distinctive gates and a strange reputation.

[As previously mentioned, trespassing is not fun and it is not a joke. Please do not do it. Years later, to spice up the story, you might want to tell people that you snuck in, but for all the obvious reasons, do not actually break the law in the name of a good story…because you might end up telling a much less pleasant story about the consequences of breaking the law.]

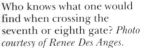

Who knows what one would find when crossing the seventh or eighth gate? *Photo courtesy of Renee Des Anges.*

Chapter Twelve
Rehoboth and Other Eerie Environs

The Redheaded Hitchhiker

Of all the ghosts in Boston, certainly one of the best known and scariest, along with the Lady in Black, is the Redheaded Hitchhiker of Route 44. No other creature of the night in Massachusetts or any other haunted location deserves the kind of warnings that must be given about a particular stretch of Route 44. In the same way that one should flee if they see Melanie Lanier, the Confederate woman who is still searching Boston and the rest of Massachusetts for her soldier husband that she inadvertently helped kill, the Redheaded Hitchhiker is not a spirit that anyone should try to find. The best solution is to avoid Route 44 whenever possible.

On that strip of road in Rehoboth, the ghost of a man with red hair has been trying to catch a ride for almost forty years. The Redheaded Hitchhiker has been spotted taking shortcuts through the woods and has even been reported standing dead center in the road waiting for a car and its unwitting driver to speed their way right through him. Even people driving Route 44 quickly, despite the trees flashing by in a blur, have gotten clear views of the Redheaded Hitchhiker. No one knows who the hitchhiker is, but they know that he is best avoided. Locals love to speak of his strange menace because the stories are fun to tell, but none of them want to come face-to-face with the Redheaded Hitchhiker.

None of the deaths reported in the area can be matched up with the man's physical appearance, though there have been many unsuccessful attempts to uncover the hitchhiker's identity. He is usually lean and muscular, over six feet tall and almost always has a beard that matches his red hair. Other aspects of his appearance have subtle changes. His hair is sometimes seen as long and scraggly and other times his hair is well groomed and swept back. The Redheaded Hitchhiker is most often sighted wearing jeans and a red flannel shirt with the red shirt sometimes left untucked.

He is usually reported to be in his forties. The easiest ways to recognize the Redheaded Hitchhiker is in his flat, sullen, or lifeless eyes and in his angry but bemused sneer. He is often reported to be smoking a cigarette when first seen and then the smoldering cigarette butt is left behind when he vanishes. Ghostly hitchhikers always vanish. It is the nature of ghostly hitchhikers. If they don't vanish, they're not ghosts.

The Redheaded Hitchhiker almost always appears to people who are driving alone. The most common scenario is for him to be lurking near the side of the road or even standing in the middle of the road. The Redheaded Hitchhiker is then either struck or wants a ride. If he makes it into the car, the Redheaded Hitchhiker will vanish soon after getting inside, often after a bit of nondescript chitchat or a carefully worded warning.

Once he vanishes, a low chuckle, hysterical maniacal laughter, or mocking taunts are often heard. Car batteries have been known to die and the laughter continues as if from the car's radio even when the battery has been completely drained and the electrical systems become inoperable. He has even been known to appear, without warning, as a shadow in the rearview mirror.

The only rumor that attempts to explain his identity is the story of a farmer who was struck by a vehicle while changing a tire. There are also stories of earlier sightings near Wilmarth Bridge Road and Redway Plain—but the origin of the legend is generally unknown. Rehoboth is often considered the most haunted locale in Massachusetts. Rehoboth is fairly near Providence, Rhode Island, and the area is also known for deep and impenetrable fog. Rehoboth also has many cemeteries, more than seems warranted for such a small town, and many are comprised of only a handful of scattered tombstones in unusual areas. The Hitchhiker could be trying to travel from one to another for all that is really understood. The Rehoboth Village Cemetery is considered to be inhabited by the living dead, but the Redheaded Hitchhiker is the entity to be worried about.

Dozens have seen him, most often in the autumn months. Boston proper and Salem are certainly more important, historically, in terms of Spooky, Creepy Boston—but Rehoboth is the current hot spot. It is where ghosts are afoot in the present day. You probably shouldn't go there; it might be bad.

Ghostly hitchhikers are, of course, commonplace in the United States of America—but few are seen as consistent in recent years as the Redheaded Hitchhiker. It should be stressed that one must beware with this particular type of undead or paranormal creature. The hitchhiker is known to be dangerous and should be avoided. Police officers have reportedly warned people away from the area that is sometimes called the "Bridgewater Triangle." From Seekonk to Rehoboth has been the Redheaded Hitchhiker's primary territory for almost twenty years now.

It is best to avoid Route 44 at night if one is driving along the Sekonk and Rehoboth miles. There are reports that honking one's horn three times increases the likelihood of encountering the hitchhiker, but such behavior is strenuously discouraged.

The Bridgewater Triangle

Ah, triangles! What would the paranormal researcher do without them? One of the best ways to make sense of the Fortean events, ghost stories, dark histories, and inexplicable geographical formations is simply to draw a perimeter around some cluster of events and reports and dig for a little folklore to perhaps explain it all. The Bridgewater Triangle was first named by Loren Coleman in the book *Mysterious America* back in 1983, but the mysterious events in the 200-square mile area have a much older provenance.

The towns of Rehoboth, Abington, and Freetown mark the points of the triangle, which contains Hockomock Swamp, the second largest wetland in Massachusetts at over 6000 acres. The swamp was used as a fortress by Wampanoag and also housed the forces of the Native American leader King Philip during his war against the settlers. Hockomock means "the place where spirits dwell" and has for 300 years resisted various attempts at draining. Various spook lights and wills o' the wisp are commonly spotted in the area, probably thanks to swamp gas—methane build-ups common in pools of stagnant water in which organic matter (vegetable or animal) decays. It is likely these bursts of phosphorescent light that gave the large swamp its Native American name, and which to this day helps feed the area's reputation as a paranormal hotspot. There is, however, more going on in the swamp, and in the Bridgewater Triangle, than the occasional burp of swamp gas.

The swamp is archeologically rich and has been the site of human habitation for perhaps as long as 9000 years. Other things live in the swamp too—both hunting and trapping remain common in the area. Civilian Conservation Corps workers and other trusted sources have reported out-of-place animals including black panthers, giant snakes, and very large turtles in the area. While game and other animals are very common in the fecund environment, perhaps not all of those animals are…known to science. *The Boston Globe* reported in 2005 stories of, "vicious, giant dogs with red eyes seen ravenously sinking their fangs into the throats of ponies; a flying creature that resembled a pterodactyl, the dinosaur that could fly…[and] a shaggy half-man, half-ape seen shuffling through the woods." The great winged creatures are often referred to as thunderbirds, based on the Native American folklore local to the area. It wouldn't be unusual at all for a very active area to have either unknown species of animals, unusual specimens of known beasts, or simply easily confused or credulous witnesses. However, one of the most common sightings—that of the shambling "skunk ape," which was even spotted by professional fur trapper John Baker in the 1990s cannot be so easily dismissed. There are no apes or even monkeys native to the area, and bears are not known to live in the swamp or walk upright for any extended period of time. (Nor would an experienced woodsman like Baker make such an elementary error.) What is out in the swamp?

Whatever it is, it may be a carnivore. Cattle mutilations have been found in the Triangle, specifically in the Fall River and Freetown errors, and police reports at the time suggested that the mutilations appeared to be ritual in manner. In 2002, a spate of sightings of unmarked black helicopters in Rehoboth and elsewhere in the triangle were reported. These haven't been connected to the typical sort of political paranoia that usually accompanies such reports. Perhaps someone's pet genetic project got loose in the woods and a few copters were sent out in the hope of spotting the beast?

Such storytelling can be interesting, and in the end is little different than the creation of the Bridgewater Triangle in the first place. The swamp gives the area an air of the wild, and even offers special effects for a variety of both spiritual and UFO sightings. The towns of the area tend to be on the small side, with little light pollution. The black skies at night are the perfect background for Ganzfield hallucinations—visions manifested by the brain when confronted with a visual field of a

single color. The brain amplifies "neural noise" in an attempt to differentiate anything possible from the single stimulus of a pitch black night. And then, UFOs, or ghostly canoes paddled by long dead Wampanoag appear. Such hallucinations can also be aural, which may explain the phantom train lines heard in the area.

Black skies at night are the perfect background for Ganzfield hallucinations.

The drawing of the triangle itself is a way of creating order from chaos. Clearly, any 200 square mile stretch of land, especially one that has been populated for hundreds of years, is going to have its fair share of stories. Indeed, there are single parks in Boston proper, such as the Common, that can beat out the so-called Bridgewater Triangle in spookiness per square foot. The Triangle allows us to generate narratives based on the swamp, and to make sense of the many and varied paranormal events that have been recorded in the surrounding areas. In the same way the haunted swamp has been used to give the area its dark reputation, our attempt to tie together the very modern events—cattle mutilations and black helicopters—with the older man-ape sightings, just serves to further the legend of the area through the creation of a seemingly consistent and perhaps plausible story.

Other Areas in Rehoboth

The Hornbine School

The Hornbine School is a one-room school from 1845. It is a white clapboard schoolhouse that has been the locus of a wide range of paranormal activity. Class has been heard in session even when the school is empty in the middle of the night. Strange furry creatures have scurried around inside and outside of the structure. Glowing orbs have been seen dancing in the night air.

The school was slightly enlarged in the 1920s but was only used until the late 1930s. It is disturbing, and another sign that Rehoboth is particularly possessed, to think that children are still heard so many years after the schoolhouse was used. The building was refurbished and repaired in 1968 as part of the celebrations for the 325th anniversary of the town. That renovation seems to be what triggered the wide array of events, which means that the ghosts are the haunted spirits of children who have remained trapped there for over seventy-five years.

At least one witness claims to have seen a teacher dressed in clothing from the 1920s and delivering a lecture to eager and wide-eyed students. The teacher glared at the witness for disturbing the class. Thinking it was a reenactment, the witness went into the schoolhouse to apologize for poor manners and the room was, of course, empty. One cannot even begin to imagine what dark lessons were being presented.

Crystal Springs School

Another school is known for a more recent grisly tragedy. The Department of Youth Services has a special school, the Crystal Springs School, for residential treatment of troubled youth. Staffers have heard strange noises and have seen an elderly woman, a young boy, a man in his twenties, and glowing balls of white light that may even be connected to the lights of the Hornbine School.

The glowing balls of light and the unrecognized man his twenties have both been reported to pass through closed and locked wooden doors. The man has only made a few appearances over a short time period, wearing a bomber jacket and his hair cut in a mullet. He vanishes when spoken to and is almost certainly a recent death or someone who was buried in the nearby cemetery but who has adopted more current attire now that he is back from the dead.

Anawan Rock

Finally, there is Anawan Rock. It is also along the dangerous Route 44 and is where colonists captured the Wampanoag Native American leader Chief Anawan in King Philip's War. Anawan Rock is a large and steep rock by the edge of a swamp. While several people have reported that they have heard whispered Algonquin words coming from thin air, Anawan Rock is best known for its deep and pervasive sense of melancholy. There have only been those whispered words and the great emptiness for most, but a few also claim to have seen misty apparitions navigating between the nearby headstones. The simplest solution is to try to avoid these spots in Rehoboth, because, at least at this time, it is the most haunted place in Massachusetts.

The Houghton Mansion in North Adams

The address 172 Church Street in North Adams is one of the most haunted mansions in all of New England. Once the dwelling of the mayor of North Adams, Albert Charles Houghton, in the beginning of the 20th century, the Houghton Mansion is now home to a Masonic lodge. It is a stately Neo-Classical Revival mansion with Greek flourishes.

The tragedy that sparked the paranormal occurrences that emanate from the Houghton Mansion building occurred in 1911. Mayor Houghton, his daughter Mary, a female friend of the family, Sybil Hutton, and the family's chauffeur, John Widders, were in an accident where the Pierce-Arrow automobile they were riding in flipped.

People were standing in the road and Widders had to swerve to dodge another vehicle that itself dodged the pedestrians. A soft shoulder of gravel gave way under the car when the Pierce-Arrow swerved. John Widders and Mayor Houghton survived, and indeed were hardly injured, but the two women died when the car turned over. For Sybil, her demise occurred at the scene when she was crushed and then thrown from the car as the vehicle tumbled down a deep embankment. For Mary, she remained in the car as it rolled over and over down the embankment and then came to the end of her life at the North Adams Hospital a few hours later.

On the next day, John Widders committed suicide by shooting himself in the head in the cellar of the barn behind the mansion. Widders had always been close to Mary and he saw himself as guilty and accountable for her death. Mayor Albert Houghton was also scarred by the tragedy of losing his daughter, though he appears to have been less shaken up by the self-murder of his long-time driver. Houghton mourned for his dead daughter until he died in the mansion from a stroke, about three years after Mary's death. It is said that Mary had promised to never marry and to care for her father's health in his old age. Without her to accompany him in the final years of his life, he faded.

Starting at Mary Houghton's death, mysterious supernatural events have happened at the Houghton Mansion and on its grounds. The Masons of the lodge have heard footsteps that could not be explained in any rational way. There are reports of knocks and crying female voices heard in empty rooms. There have even been accounts of people feeling the touch of an unseen presence or getting chills or feelings of numbness through their bodies. Some feel peace upon entering the building, but others report a weight of tragedy and sadness coming over them.

The Houghton Mansion is also where the Berkshire Paranormal Group is located. Because of their presence, a great deal of photographic and EVP evidence have been collected. That group continues to investigate and allow research to be done on site. It is unclear who of four possibilities (Mary Houghton, her father, John Widders or even Sybil Hutton) is haunting the Houghton Mansion—but it seems clear that the matter will continue to be investigated by the Berkshire Paranormal Group and others.

North Houghton Mansion
172 Church Street
North Adams, MA
(413) 652-0324
For Paranormal Researchers: JMantello@msn.com

Colonial Inn in Concord

Room number 24 of the Colonial Inn in Concord, Massachusetts is haunted. Gray mist that appears in the shape of a human being floats around the room. It is unclear whether the specter is pacing or trying to escape. Paranormal investigators have collected various bits of evidence and Room 24 is clearly still a hot zone for ghostly activity. In the center of Concord, in Monument Square, the hotel has a long and storied history dating back to before the Revolutionary War, but the haunting of Room 24 is much more recent.

When noted physician Doctor Minot treated injured soldiers during the revolution and when the house was converted into a boarding house, there were most likely traumatic events that laid the ground for the current manifestation. The room was part of the original house that Dr. Minot, both a physician and a soldier, built in 1716.

As far as is known or can be determined, the first occurrence was in 1966. M.P. and Judith Fellenz were honeymooning, traveling to the Colonial Inn from Highland Falls, New York. One can imagine the rustic or quaint feel that the newlyweds dreamed of as they traveled through New England. Instead, as they departed Judith looked unspeakably pale and said few words.

Two weeks later, a letter from Judith Fellenz arrived, addressed to Innkeeper Loring Grimes. Judith Fellenz told the innkeeper that she had always considered herself mentally stable but that she was now unsure of her own sanity because she had witnessed a ghost in Room 24 on the night of June 14th. Judith Fellenz explained that she was too embarrassed to tell Innkeeper Grimes when she and her husband left the Colonial Inn.

Mrs. Fellenz had been too terrified to bring up the haunting and she and Mr. Fellenz had continued on their honeymoon—but she wrote the letter because she needed to know if she was the only one who had experienced the phenomenon.

Mrs. Fellenz reported that she had been awoken by the spirit in the middle of the night, a sense that an unknown presence was in the room. She opened her eyes and saw a shadowy gray figure floating over her bed. The ghost was indistinct and amorphous but clearly suggested a human form. The ghost remained motionless for a moment and then floated to the front of the bed, rippling in the air as it came nearer. Then the apparition vanished. Mrs. Fellenz said, in her letter, that she was so terrified that she was unable to move or scream, even though she had wanted to do both. She wanted a rational explanation and was convinced that there was no explanation that she could ascertain.

Colonial Inn
48 Monument Square
Concord, MA 01742
(978) 369-9200

Conclusion
Strange and Deranged

"Hiccory, diccory, dock,
The mouse run up the clock;
The clock struck one, and down he run,
Hiccory, diccory, dock."

Hiccory Diccory Dock
Mother Goose Nursery Rhyme, 1833

As one can imagine, Boston Harbor is home to one of the most fearsome ghosts on the Eastern Seaboard. The Boston Harbor was crucial to protecting the city from attack in the Revolutionary War. Given the crucial role of Boston as a port city that helped win the country's freedom, it stands to reason that Fort Warren, located on the 28-acre George's Island, would be home to one of the most-repeated tales in the region. Knowing what could happen when the light went out seems enough to keep someone from wanting to stop saving ships just because they happen to be deceased. This is like how the tenth floor of the Omni Parker Hotel has also been known to have been filled with the sound of squeaking rocking chairs even though the hotel has checked everywhere and has been unable to find a single rocking chair in the entire building. The tenth floor has had floating orbs of light that have been witnessed by several bellmen.

Stories abound in Boston town. The streets of Boston are rumored to have been laid out by old cow paths because it is a city that evolved before cars were first invented. Anyone who has driven the streets will testify that they swirl and curve in ways that only locals can comprehend. The truth is probably that topography and the organic nature of the development (long before urban planning came into vogue) make the roads feel so random.

Boston was originally just a peninsula, a delta where three rivers came together. Over time, given the rivers and hills, the streets were laid out based out on connecting people to shipping and commerce centers that have changed over time—but cows make for a better story.

Mother Goose is probably the same. The folklore and the truth are intermingled to enough of a degree that the stories do more good than harm. That is all that I have tried to offer with all of these stories. The best guess is that Isaac Goose, after Mary Goose died, married Elizabeth Foster Goose. Then Isaac Goose died and Elizabeth Foster Goose moved in with Thomas Fleet. From there, truth and the threads of the stories probably deviate. What is most likely is that the stories themselves came from almost everywhere. Thomas Fleet gathered the stories and published them in 1720. The name Mother Goose was already in the ethers in Europe and it fit his mother-in-law. Multiple sources were combined into Boston legend. Fleet's historic first was probably that he was the first to attribute an American book to Mother Goose. Some claim that Elizabeth Foster Goose, also buried in the Boston Common graveyard, was the original "Mother Goose" of fairy tales and folklore, while others point to the stone of Mary Goose, who died in 1690. Those of us who have studied such topics know that everything is true and that nothing is forbidden.

If we picture the founders of Boston, they are in short cloaks, silk stockings and doublets, but the colors are dour. Plaited ruffs with a furlong of linen, the original name of Boston was Trimountain (which lives on with "Tremont" Street) because of Beacon Hill and two others that were flattened long ago: Copp's Hill and Fort Hill. The oldest tombstone that was marked in Copp's Hill Cemetery was from 1625, before Boston was even settled. It is a strange region that so many call home. The legends of the mental institutions and the film *Session 9* end up telling the same story and trying to discern which version of the story came first leads down the road to madness.

Mother Goose, Insanity, and Shipwrecks, these are the Boston we love. Ghosts linger because they are mysteries. They live on because there are facts and details that we cannot put our name on. Souls do not always pass through, sometimes they stop and pause and look around. We are ghosts and we are monsters. We want to believe in monsters, but sometimes we are tossed into a hideous abyss where it is hard to make sense using the limited boundaries of reality. When doors swing open or slam shut by themselves, when bells in cupolas ring on their own, we are trying to describe that which it is hard to describe. When the investigators of an organization like the researchers of New England's Queen City Paranormal set up infrared and thermal cameras, when they set up electromagnetic frequency detectors or recording equipment, they are trying to find deep and powerful forms of truth. We all want to prove something. We all want to comprehend the remarkable. The creak of the floor is the desire to understand what goes on around us.

The moon rises on the Atlantic waters and we begin to feel disoriented. We are in a different land. The spooky and creepy powers of Massachusetts are terrifying and alluring and they date back as far as Boston stories go. Some become lost in the desolate madness and illusion and some learn to make peace with the ghosts around them. The fact that two female killers, Jane Tappan and Lizzie Borden, appear in this volume says something about Boston and its eerie environs, as does The Lady in Black. Tappan and Borden are much better known and understood than the Boston Strangler. This is where we live and who we are.

In trying to make sense of how these stories live on and leave us frightened, it was worthwhile to talk to Mike Krausert, of the *Terror on the Fox* haunted attraction in Green Bay, Wisconsin, and Director of both *Spooky World* and *Nightmare New England* (one of America's largest Halloween Scream Parks in Litchfield, New Hampshire). He is one of the most prominent figures in horror and haunted attractions in the United States. He captured the essence of Massachusetts and haunting when he said:

"People celebrate Halloween a lot more here [in New England] than in Wisconsin or maybe even any other part of the country. It has a lot to do with Salem and the witch trials and that's why we try to connect the story we created for the park to Salem."

Here is Mike Krausert of the *Terror on the Fox* haunted attraction in Green Bay, Wisconsin, and Director of both *Spooky World* and *Nightmare New England* (one of America's largest Halloween Scream Parks in Litchfield, New Hampshire)—and a friend.

Like most of New England's folklore, Halloween blurs the line between life and death. *Nightmare New England* focuses on detail and raising the stakes to make their haunted attraction bigger, scarier and more terrifying each year. An example is their burial simulator "ride" where a person climbs inside a coffin and hears the sounds of their funeral and trip to the graveyard, even smelling the flowers, exhaust, dirt and then decay of their final voyage. With 120 actors a night and with several thousand visitors on the peak nights just before Halloween, *Nightmare New England* and *Spooky World* are evidence of how, as Krausert said, in New England, "Halloween has more of a history here, more deeply rooted." Not unlike a ghost story, "it's like a theater production, you want everything to happen when it's supposed to happen. You want everything to look good. You want people to leave enjoying what they saw."

Nightmare New England and Spooky World
Mike Krausert, Director of Operations
454 Charles Bancroft Highway
Litchfield, NH
03052
Website: www.nightmarenewengland.com
Phone: (603)913-9099

In many ways, Boston folklore is interlinked with Salem. Many of the legends and stories have variants that connect to Salem. The folklore of Boston would certainly be different if it were not for Salem being such a cultural touchstone. Salem is what gives the fearsome tales of Boston so many textures and resonances. If the physiological finds you, it is likely to be pain. An itch, a burn, a chill. If you become indoctrinated into darkness, married to the night, you will see that you are merely one with existence. We are all acolytes to something. Doorways open. Crossing over is what thresholds are for. Making that dark pact brings possession and power. Demons bite, scratch, and stick pins in order to extract the promises. Strangulations and incomprehensible mutterings still occur all the time. With a haunted attraction, you know that the ticket is in your pocket. With ghosts, you never asked for these things to happen.

Haunted alleyways abound in Spooky Creepy Boston.

Haley A. Wright, of Queen City Paranormal of New Hampshire described paranormal investigations as, "Our main goal is to help people. I was in a situation where I was in an apartment that we felt was haunted. Where do you go? It's not like you can look in the yellow pages and find a phone number." Who are you gonna call? It is hard to find certainty in matter of the paranormal. People come to these haunted locations freaked out and wanting to find answers—yet all the moon does is laugh. Haley pointed out that most of the requests for ghost hunting come in through email nowadays. Much of the research into ghosts is found online now. Wright described this phenomenon as,

It's a young science. It's like anything that started out. Everything seemed crazy. People used to think the world was flat. People thought you were crazy if you said the world was round. It's the same thing with this. Right now, everyone's going to think we're crazy until enough well-known people come out with facts. A lot of scientists look down on parapsychology but it's getting better because more prominent scientists are starting to look into it and they're starting to get results from experiments they're doing.

Was that a faucet turning on? Any study of ghosts is a case study of one. There is no control group. Summing up how the dark traditions of Gothic literature connect to New England, distinguished scholar Dr. Faye Ringel, in pointing out that the first package bus tour in U.S. history was to Salem also mentioned that,

> There's always been this really interesting tension, actually—when you talk about the Gothic aesthetic—there's the tension between those who only get a frisson from the literary style of the retelling and those who want the truth. It has been since the very beginning.

Haley A. Wright of Queen City Paranormal of New Hampshire is dedicated to helping people in matters involving the paranormal. *Photo courtesy of Haley A. Wright of Queen City Paranormal of New Hampshire.*

Shown here are devices used by Queen City Paranormal of
New Hampshire. *Photo courtesy of Haley A. Wright of Queen City
Paranormal of New Hampshire.*

Queen City Paranormal of New Hampshire

c/o Haley Wright
P.O. Box 224
Candia, NH 03034
Website: http://www.queencityghosts.com/
Phone: (603)703-9964

Dr. Ringel spoke of how H.P. Lovecraft used his new monstrous entities because the old monsters no longer had the same influences that they once did. Our earliest explorers of New England believed in mermaids and unicorns. How are we any different with our ghosts and specters?

In bringing this book to an end, I cannot help but remember the wise words of Joe Louis, "The Brown Bomber," heavyweight boxing champion of the world: "I'm telling my wife the other day that when I die I only want one word on my tombstone. I want 'Even' on it. The world doesn't owe me nothing and I hope I don't owe it nothing. So we're even. That's the way I want it. That's the good way."

Pacts with dark forces are often brought on by ourselves. If you are going out to investigate the paranormal, you should bring friends. If you go by yourself, no one will believe when you tell them that a gigantic winged creature with dripping fangs dragged you twenty yards before hurling you against a headstone unless there are witnesses.